The final step in the ultimate journey
to love, inner peace, and personal fulfillment...

TRAVELING THE ROYAL ROAD:
Mastering the Tarot

The revealing guide that unlocks
the Tarot's furthest doors and leads you
to the most detailed and sophisticated
understanding of the cards' powers of enlightenment!

TRAVELING THE ROYAL ROAD:
Mastering the Tarot

Nancy Shavick

BERKLEY BOOKS, NEW YORK

TRAVELING THE ROYAL ROAD: MASTERING THE TAROT

A Berkley Book / published by arrangement with
the author

PRINTING HISTORY
Berkley edition / April 1992

ISBN: 0-425-13246-3

A BERKLEY BOOK ® TM 757,375
Berkley Books are published by The Berkley Publishing Group,
200 Madison Avenue, New York, New York 10016.
The name "BERKLEY" and the "B" logo
are trademarks belonging to Berkley Publishing Corporation.

PRINTED IN THE UNITED STATES OF AMERICA

10 9 8 7 6 5 4 3 2 1

This book is dedicated to all
peace workers
in search of happy miracles

<u>Traveling the Royal Road: Mastering the Tarot</u> is volume three of the Tarot trilogy that began with <u>The Tarot</u>, which was followed by <u>The Tarot Reader</u>. This latest book shows further methods for gaining greater accuracy and meaning from readings. It presents actual readings that I have given to inquirers, more information on interpreting Tarot readings, guidelines for setting up your own Tarot journal, and my thoughts on the Tarot, accompanied by a discussion of the Tarot decks available today.

Instructions for using all the Tarot spreads mentioned in <u>Traveling the Royal Road</u> can be found in my first two books, <u>The Tarot</u> and <u>The Tarot Reader</u>. All spread work in this volume is based on spreads illustrated in the first two volumes.

Part One of <u>Traveling the Royal Road</u>, "Notes on the Tarot Deck and Its History," presents a brief history of the Tarot tradition and describes many of the different mass-produced Tarot decks that are currently for sale. This section will help you sort out how to choose a deck from nearly one hundred

Tarot packs that can be purchased. Part One also includes a running commentary that reveals my thoughts on the impact and benefits of card readings.

"The Tarot Journal" is the focus of Part Two of this book. Here you will find advice on how and why you should set up a Tarot journal to keep a record of your readings and to evaluate their validity over time. This chapter demonstrates sample methods for writing down many of the spreads from <u>The Tarot</u> and <u>The Tarot Reader</u>.

Part Three, "Further Ideas about Interpreting a Tarot Reading," answers many of the most commonly asked questions about Tarot readings such as how often the cards should be read; how long a reading takes to come true, and what hazards lie in speculation through the Tarot. This section shows you how to prepare yourself mentally for a reading and tells you why some readings fail. Part Three ends with some new hints for spread interpretation.

Part Four, "Tarot Cards in Particular Positions of the Grand Cross

Spread," is an exercise in adjusting the definition of a card to precisely fit a position of the Grand Cross. Part Four offers many examples of what a card means in a specific Grand Cross placement.

Part Five, "Seven Tarot Readings," presents my method of reading the cards for an inquirer using the subject-combination and the Grand Cross and Four Card spreads. These transcribed readings will give you many clues for synthesizing a Tarot reading that examines an issue through two Tarot spreads.

Contents

NOTES ON THE TAROT DECK AND ITS HISTORY

The Tarot is historically connected to the mythology and iconography of many diverse cultures, and reading the cards is a practice that is understood globally as a universal language. The 78-card Tarot deck accentuates principles common to the symbolic dogma of of numerous belief systems throughout the record of humanity and highlights archetypal circumstances that are shared by all civilizations at all times.

The Tarot cards are allegorical pictorial representations rooted in ancient Greek and Egyptian legends, alchemy, astrology, numerology, free-masonry and the royal and Gypsy cultures of southern Europe. They comprise an eccentric and often obscure metaphysical system that classifies the behavior of the cosmos as it influences people, events and circumstances here on earth. The imagery of the traditional Tarot deck glorifies moral and spiritual wisdom through the depiction of occupational figures from different hierarchical strata of society dressed in costumes from the Middle

Ages and the enigmatic characters that portray planetary entities (Sun, Moon, Star and Universe or World cards), courtly medieval personalities (Juggler, Fool, Hermit, Emperor, Empress, King, Queen, Knight and Page), ancient virtues (Strength, Justice, Temperance), Greek and Egyptian mythological references (Juno or High Priestess, Jupiter or Priest or Hierophant, Magus or Magician, Osiris [Emperor] and Isis [Empress], Sun, Chariot, Hanged Man) and Biblical concepts (Devil, Last Judgement [Judgement], Pope, Female Pope [Juno or High Priestess], Marriage [Lovers] and Tower of Babel [Tower]).

The cards are generally believed to be a relic of the ancient Egyptian worship of Thoth and the early Italian veneration of Mercury as well as the Greek tradition of honoring Hermes. All these gods were considered messengers who ruled communication and had a sacred and divinatory purpose as does the Tarot, which originally was a means for discovering the intentions of the gods through the guidance of a reading.

The Tarot cards form a bible of ageless wisdom presented in picture form and describing eternal truths about the way the universe works. The Tarot is a philosophical code of spiritual law that explains how our personal Karma controls our cycles of activity and change as we proceed in fulfilling our preordained destinies. The cards are personifications of lessons taught by natural metaphysical and psychological principles whose meaning is understood as you gain awareness of how the drama of your conscious reality connects to your ever-evolving subconscious intelligence, which depicts the greater picture of the purpose of your soul.

The cards are considered the sum total of enlightenment available to us as the card system defines all levels of physical, emotional, intellectual or creative states as represented by the definitions of the 78 Tarot cards. The cards identify every type of feeling, incident, characteristic of humanity and metaphysical truth eternally found within the repetitive cycles of the universe. The Tarot reflects the ever-changing emphasis of your activities, whether harmonious or chaotic, as you work to attune your life to the chord of heavenly law. Readings can help you purify your negative and destructive tendencies and lead you toward choices that will fulfill you spiritually and make you happier with your existential situation.

The Tarot cards are a textbook for raising your consciousness by discovering the will of divine guidance, which always explains the reasons for your confusion, unhappiness or wariness and urges you to evolve and become stronger so you can make the most positive choices on the path of sacred liberation and find your individual freedom through your journey along the royal road.

Tarot readings reveal the true spirit of each soul by relaying the past, present and future to determine obstacles and opportunities and gain greater independence, awareness and joy in the present. You use the Tarot to acquire insight into your talents, abilities and personality, gain clarity of your career direction and expand the boundaries of your potential. In the best sense, a reading should be a private method of deliberation where you form your own opinion by maintaining privacy and making decisions for yourself. The reading is a tool for thinking things over and working out your problems in a self-reliant manner. The very act of reading the cards forces you to sit down and center your attention on finding viable, successful solutions. The reading is never the final word on what will happen; it merely illustrates the options you have concerning a particular matter and what sort of behavior you can expect from yourself and others. A reading only reflects the current schedule of destiny, which can be altered in the future, by showing what is likely to come to pass later on. Therefore you can know what in all probability will occur, which enables you to influence the outcome of your fate by fortifying your attitude and initiative toward a preferred result. The Tarot can also assist you by re-creating events from long ago through the cards that land in the past placements of the spread, allowing you to look back in time and learn from a previous experience as it relates to your present drama.

The Tarot is a science of observation that requires you to remember what the cards mean and utilize your intuition to piece the story of the reading together by your interpretation of the spread. Through the analysis of the reading, your conscious and subconscious minds glean information mirrored in the Tarot spread. In this way, the cards help you view a particular action in relation to the moral and philosophical framework of the universe and not as an isolated incomprehensible event that is only one piece of the puzzle that depicts your current sojourn on earth. The Tarot enlightens you morally, ideologically, psychologically and spiritually through profound and powerful readings that serve as points of clarification to propel you into action and steer your heart, mind, soul and body toward achieving what you came here to accomplish.

Readings can help you align yourself with your deepest dreams while you become more self-reliant about choosing which way to go in life. They can show with uncanny accuracy what is happening to you at the time of the reading and what will happen in the future. In this way, readings give you a sense of direction by assisting you in understanding the way things work so that you can increase your awareness and thus make a better life for yourself as well as others.

A perfect Tarot reading is a magical session where the card reader uses the deck as a tool for gleaning knowledge from other realms in order to gain insight. The reader, the deck, the collective unconscious and the inquirer must all be functioning on the same wavelength for this miraculous meeting of minds to take place. Until you reach this stage of card reading, utilize The Tarot and The Tarot Reader to identify how each

card in a spread should be interpreted.
Eventually you will come to a point where
you will remember what the 78 cards
mean and will no longer have to rely
heavily on the books, although you may
want to refer to them periodically.

The information that comes through
the reading is extremely valuable to the
development of your soul because the
inner voice that speaks to you when you
read the cards is the best guidance to
be found anywhere. A clear reading will
always push you toward who or what
is really right for you based on your
destiny requirements that your higher
self is aware of but your personality cannot grasp as easily due to your karma
tripping you up as you try to move along
your proper path in life. This explains
why you have so much difficulty getting
what you want when you want it, because the time, person, place or group is
not crucial to your journey along the
royal road. The Tarot reading can
also help you change old patterns and
habits that are comfortable but uncomfortable at the same time. Although you
are discontented, you have trouble seeing

your destructive tendencies and do nothing about replacing deadening activities with satisfying, simple and natural alternatives.

The relationship that develops between you and your Tarot deck should reinforce your belief in the ability of the cards to help you comprehend the spiritual story behind your existence. A good reading will always fill you up with positivity and hope for a better future for yourself and others. Tarot readings never fail to tell the truth to an inquiring individual who desires to see things as they absolutely are. The cards continually direct you toward the highest and the best the world has to offer, so that you can make good use of your incarnation and leave behind a history of creative acts that adds to the harmony of the spheres by being in alignment with the balance of the cosmos.

For the most part, the standard 78-card Tarot deck has survived virtually unchanged for at least five hundred years. Tarot cards are currently used for readings all over the world, and since the

1960's millions of Tarot decks have been sold. Today over one hundred different decks are mass-produced for distribution in the United States alone as artists continue to reinterpret the imagery of the cards at a time when the Tarot is undergoing a renaissance of interest worldwide that does not seem to be abating. The Tarot is more popular internationally than ever before and has strong audiences all over the United States and Canada as well as Europe, Japan, South America, India, Australia, New Zealand and many other places. In almost every major city in the world, you can find Tarot classes, readers and decks available for sale, often in more than one location.

This popularity has resulted in the creation of an assortment of decks, each with slight modifications in the symbolic pictures that adorn the faces of the cards. When choosing a deck, everybody is influenced by different aspects of the Tarot deck. Some people are attracted to antique classic decks such as the Marseilles deck, the old woodblock-printed decks from France, Italy and Switzerland

and the the gilded Visconti-Sforza deck
that dates from the fifteenth century.
Others choose modern interpretations of
the traditional deck, including the
Rider-Waite deck, 1JJ Swiss Tarot, the
Hanson-Roberts deck, the Royal Fez
Moroccan deck, the Thoth deck, Salvador
Dali's Tarot deck, the Art Nouveau
Tarot deck, the Angel Tarot, the Morgan-
Greer Tarot deck, the Knapp-Hall Tarot
and the Sacred Rose Tarot. More recent
decks, like the Motherpeace Tarot deck
and the Voyager Tarot deck, offer new
approaches to the visual aspect of the
cards. Many packs are now available
that have cultural or ethnic images on
the faces. Among them are the Ukiyoe
Tarot deck (Japanese), the Chinese
Tarot deck, the Merlin Tarot deck, the
Native American Tarot deck, the Egyptian
Tarot deck, Tarot of the Ages(multi-cultural),
the Norse Tarot deck (Viking legends),
the Mayan Tarot deck and the Medicine
Woman Tarot. Tarot theme decks are
numerous: the Jungian Tarot deck,
the Herbal Tarot deck, the Tarot of
the Cat People, the Puppet Tarot deck
and the Robot Tarot. Any or all of these

decks can be used in conjunction with <u>The Tarot</u>, <u>The Tarot Reader</u> and <u>Traveling the Royal Road</u>.

Some readers use a variety of decks for doing Tarot readings while others like to read with only one type of deck. The artwork on the cards is a major factor in drawing people to a particular Tarot deck. The image on a card influences how you interpret it, and many readers prefer to ultilize the simplest, least cluttered decks. When you begin to read you may find it helpful to start with a highly animated deck like the classic Rider-Waite where the pip cards are brought to life in scenes depicting human activity instead of starting out with a deck like the 1JJ Swiss that has two crossed swords depicting the two of swords, for example. The two of swords in the Rider-Waite pack shows a blindfolded woman balancing two swords on her shoulders as she sits on a bench with her back to the sea under a crescent moon. Some decks attribute extremely complex associations to each card. The Church of Light Tarot deck, for example, assigns symbols of planets, numbers, Hebrew letters and zodiac signs to the 78 cards.

You may wish to buy a deck that appeals to you aesthetically, or you may select the deck that another card reader has utilized when reading your cards. You should feel comfortable with the deck and find it user-friendly when you begin to read for yourself and others. Many people receive a deck as a gift and then stick with that deck for life. Some card readers work with decks that are missing cards, with regular playing cards with suits of spades, clubs, hearts and diamonds, or even with Tarocchi decks.

In many of the newer decks, the names of the trumps and the label names of the four pip suits have been changed, as have the titles of the court cards. The following list includes the names of the Tarot decks and the modifications their creators have made on the traditional 78-card Tarot deck:

Thoth deck. Pages and kings turn into princes and princesses in this deck. All of the pip cards except the aces bear a descriptive term on the bottom of the card, such as "Peace" for the two of swords. This deck changes Justice to Adjustment, the Wheel of Fortune to Fortune, Strength to Lust, Temperance to Art and Judgement to the Aeon.

Motherpeace Tarot deck. This deck of round Tarot cards replaces the Hermit with the Crone, and the Hanged Man becomes the Hanged One. The court card titles undergo a change as the kings, queens, knights and pages of the traditional deck turn into daughters, sons, priestesses and shamans. The court cards are referred to as the Daughter of wands, the Son of wands, the Priestess of wands, the Shaman of wands, and so on.

Voyager Tarot deck. The court cards are man, woman, child and sage here. Suits are crystals (mind), cups (heart) worlds (body) and wands (spirit). The Voyager deck is composed of collages of photographs and other illustrations.

<u>Karma Tarot</u>. Juno or the High Priestess becomes Wise Woman, the Empress turns into Lilith, the Emperor is here called Osiris, and Jupiter or the Hierophant is titled the Grand Master.

<u>Herbal Tarot</u>. The Hanged Man is the Suspended Person in this deck, and the Devil is referred to as Pan.

<u>Native American Tarot deck</u>. Some changes in trump titles are Hosteen Coyote (Juggler), Corn Maiden (Juno), Medicine Woman (Empress), Council Chief (Emperor) and Shaman (Jupiter). The suits are blades (swords), pipes (wands), vessels (cups) and shields (disks). The court cards are matriarch, chief, warrior and maiden.

<u>Merlin Tarot deck</u>. The pips in this pack are called by the suit names of birds, dragons, fishes and beasts.

<u>Tarot of the Ages deck</u>. The trump cards represent Egyptian civilization. The pip suits are Vikings (swords), Africans (wands), Aztecs (cups) and East Indians

(disks).

Angel Tarot deck. Though the pip suit
titles are swords, wands, cups and
disks, the artwork of each of the pips
contains the symbols of spades, hearts,
clubs and diamonds incorporated into
the design.

Norse Tarot deck. In this pack some of
the trump titles are Balder (Fool), Odin
(Juggler), Frigga (Juno), Freya (Empress), Tyr (Emperor) and Thor
(Chariot). The court cards are kings,
queens, princesses and princes.

Cat People Tarot deck. The suits are
called rubies (swords), emeralds (wands),
topazes (cups) and sapphires (disks).
The trump cards are associated with
diamonds.

Mayan Tarot deck. Twenty of the trump
cards in this deck are called by the names
of the days of the Mayan month. The pips
are titled in five different languages:
French, English, Spanish, Italian
and German.

Knapp-Hall Tarot. The court cards are named king, queen, warrior and squire. Each trump card is inscribed with a Hebrew letter and a heraldic emblem.

Robot Tarot. All the card titles are in Italian, and the pip suits have been altered to laser (swords), nulla (wands), scarabee (cups) and luci (disks).

Medicine Woman Tarot. The four minor arcana or pip suits are called arrows, pipes, bowls and stones. The court cards are defined as exemplar, harvest lodge, totem and apprentice. Each trump card contains a single-word description across its base, such as "Harvest" for the Wheel of Fortune.

Visconti-Sforza Tarot deck. This ancient deck has some unique trump titles and stands out from the other antique decks for this very reason. The Mountebank (Juggler), the Old Man (Hermit), the Traitor (Hanged Man) and the Angel (Universe) are the titles this deck has changed. The court cards are referred to as kings, queens, knights and jacks, instead of pages.

THE TAROT JOURNAL

A Tarot journal gives you a place to record
your readings so you can refer to them
at a later date and observe how they
come to life over a period of time. Your
journal can assist you in learning more
about what the cards mean, how a reading
works and why and when it comes true.
By writing down your readings you can
see which cards are periodically prominent in or absent from your readings. You
can use your journal to catalog your own
ideas about the Tarot and chronicle any
innovative spread or card designs that
you create independently. Your journal
gives you a place to record annotated
readings that describe who or what you
think a card indicates in a spread position. You must be honest when you make
note of the information that occurs to
you logically and intuitively during the
reading so you can accurately predict
the future through the Tarot. Use your
diary to develop a truthful response to
the cards. The journal is a place to
store your self-reliant wisdom concerning the unique pattern of your personality
as it matures.

   Over the years your Tarot journal

can help you understand universal law as it is revealed through the slow, steady unfoldment typical of spiritual evolution. Having a private niche in which to establish your Tarot archive will enrich you creatively as an artist, intellectually as a problem solver, emotionally with your relationships and materially with your finances. Most of all, you will sharpen your skills as a card reader so you can give insightful readings that can heal your inquirers by presenting them with an accurate picture of their existence.

Making drawings of cards or of random images can help you comprehend their visual symbolism through the free-form associations your subconscious brings into your conscious mind as you casually sketch. Also, expressing your feelings through imaginative pictures will aid you in the release of anxiety, confusion and strife from your life as the artwork reflects back at you what is going on inside you; you are creating a revealing portrait of yourself from a stream-of-consciousness mode. If you have trouble writing down what

you think a spread means, cover a page
of your journal with doodles that can
visually explain what your logical faculties are having difficulty interpreting.

Your journal is a valuable tool that
can help you sort out the issues that constantly emerge day after day. It allows
you to witness lifetime themes that are
repeated over and over through time until
you become aware of your need to resolve
ancient conflicts with roots in your past
behavior. Your journal will be a mirror of
your entire existence as seen through the
ever-changing emphasis of the readings.
You will notice how all your readings link
together to form a continual pattern of
events, conflicts, characters and cele-
brations as you progress spiritually and
mature emotionally on every level of
your being. The past, present and future
positions of the spreads enable you to
understand the value of what has gone
before as you make peace with your past,
the importance of accepting your present
situation and learning from it, and the
drama that is likely to be waiting in the
wings of your current-stage environment.

Your Tarot journal can assist you in

resolving recurring problems if you make good use of it and regularly record your layouts. Reread your diary on occasion to glean insight from past experiences that were confusing or painful due to loss, hurt, emptiness or loneliness and which reinforced your negative self-image. Going back to old readings at a later date forces you to re-create a past that previously bewildered you. By providing answers to urgent questions about the past, present and future, your journal will help you gain wisdom and strength. If you faithfully scribble down in your personal Tarot archive the names of the cards in their spread positions and make note of what you think each reading means, you will have a lot of fun trying to match the readings to reality. You can test your card-reading ability through your journal, which holds the history of correlations between what the cards say and what happens in your life on a mental, spiritual, emotional and practical level.

The journal can be best utilized to record your immediate impression

of the significance of a reading so that
you can capture your initial intuitive
response to the cards and witness your
own train of thought as you associate
the symbolism of the reading you receive
with various people, places and things
in your day-to-day activities. Much
self-discovery will occur through your
Tarot journal as it teaches you about
the workings of your subconscious because the cards so eloquently illustrate
your personal story, with its ups and
downs and the inexplicable twists of
fate that move you along in your evolution as a spiritual being. After a while
you will become totally in tune with the
synchronicity between the readings and
what comes to pass in actuality.

Recording readings is a positive
step toward being well informed about
how to map your future by comprehending
why your existence is a certain way as
you unlock the wisdom behind the facade
of your daily spectacle. Writing down
your readings can help you reach back
in time and recall events and people
that have already faded from your
conscious memory. Because you recorded

the reading in your journal, you can view with a more mature eye things that once seemed important to you. From a distance these passing passions can be seen as archetypes in the ever-changing spiritual education played out during the course of your incarnation. Readings also enable you to reach forward into the future and gain knowledge of what is going to happen. Like a powerfully prophetic dream, a reading can be validated if you record it upon awakening while you still remember it in complete detail. Your omniscient subconscious is at work whether you are giving a reading or dreaming in a heavy REM cycle, and it is always thrilling when a reading or dream comes true in the context of your existence. If you do not write down the dream or reading, you could forget it entirely or lose the thoughts and feelings that it evoked in you. And like astrological transits, accurate Tarot readings help you visualize the people, places and events that play a dominant role in your life. Readings prepare you mentally and emotionally for what is to come and allow you to process the impact that the impending changes will have on you. When a reading comes true, make a note in your journal of how and when the prediction came to pass before your eyes.

As an added bonus, your Tarot diary will help strengthen your memory, as you will naturally retain a recollection of the cards that surfaced in spread positions on different days. This method of thinking will exercise the part of your brain designed to store and analyze such complex data. The act of reading the cards and remembering the spread will grant you more mental control, which can aid your other pursuits as you further the destiny of your soul.

Once you start giving readings to other people, you might find it helpful to use a tape recorder to capture your dialogue as you read through the spreads. Later you can listen to the reading and gain insight into how you come across as a reader. You can get an idea of whether you are insecure and hesitant about expressing your interpretation of the cards or whether you are confident, truthful and right on target with your style and technique of card reading. Tape-record readings when you feel proficient enough to give a clear, unbiased reading with a close friend sitting in as the inquirer. Initially it is easier to read for someone with whom you feel comfortable and share similar spiritual values.

Setting Up Your Journal

Choose a notebook with unlined pages of plain white paper or use sheets of paper that you can clip together or store in a folder or loose-leaf binder. You will need unlined, unadorned paper so you can write and draw freely without any visual restrictions. Turn to your journal whenever you wish to record ideas, readings or sketches of Tarot cards. It is not necessary to record every single reading that you give, though you may want to do so when you first start reading and filling your journal to increase your knowledge of the Tarot. Always jot down readings that seem especially powerful or truthful to you.

Whenever you sit down to do a

reading, grab your journal, Tarot deck and writing implement; have <u>The Tarot</u> and <u>The Tarot Reader</u> nearby for easy reference. Follow the instructions for ascertaining the significator on pages 23 through 25 of <u>The Tarot</u> and determine the subject-combination of the reading as outlined on pages 26 through 29. Record the date of the reading, the subject-combination, and the name of the spread you are using in the journal. Then write down the question(s) you brought to the reading so later on you can recall what the reading was examining. You can then put the episode into perspective in terms of the overall picture of your passage through life. Next, begin to shuffle the deck and mentally concentrate on the information you want from the reading. Lay the cards out into the spread design you wish to utilize and turn them over one at a time, interpreting them in their numerical order in the spread. Write down the number and name of each of the spread positions and the names of the cards that surface in all of the placements. Relax, take a few deep breaths and let your intuition take over as you study the imagery of the cards for clues or look up their principal meanings in the definition sections of <u>The Tarot</u> and <u>The Tarot Reader</u>. Combine the interpretation of the card with the significance of the spread position where it lands after the shuffling process.

Next, as quickly as possible, spontaneously record everything you are thinking, feeling and seeing in your imagination, jotting down the best articulation of what you are experiencing visually, intellectually and emotionally. Capture every single idea and image that occurs to you as you read through the spread. Be calm and patient while interpreting and recording a reading in your journal so you can retain as much of your original impression as you can.

Write down the spread positions in numerical order and the names of the cards that land in them, using the following suggested methods:

December 1, 1991

Grand Cross
LOVE AND MONEY

1. Self card – Universe
2. Present environment – four of wands
3. Immediate obstacle – Knight of wands
4. Hope and dream – Chariot
5. Difficulties in the past – six of swords
6. Last of the present – eight of wands
7. First of the future – Justice
8. Future environment – Knight of cups
9. Outer influence – nine of wands
10. Hope and fear – Strength
11. Outcome – three of wands

Or you could record a Grand Cross in this abbreviated manner, following the spread design found on page 35 of <u>The Tarot</u> and page 67 of this volume:

	Chariot		3 W
			Strength
8 W	Universe 4 W Kn W	Justice	
			9 W
	6 S		Kn C

Or for the Four Card Spread found on page 38 of <u>The Tarot</u>:

1. Work — Star
2. Love — six of cups
3. Trouble — ten of wands
4. Money — ten of disks

   10D   10W   6C   Star

Or for the Past, Present, Future Spread found on page 40 of <u>The Tarot</u>:

1-3. Past material — Hanged Man, six of wands and Page of cups
4-5. Present material — Star and Tower
6-8. Future material — nine of wands, Queen of disks and four of swords
9-10. Past love — Fool and the eight of wands
11-13. Present love — Empress, King of cups and Justice
14-15. Future love — Lovers and Queen of cups
16-18. Past liberation — Moon, Sun and two of swords
19-20. Present liberation — Knight of swords and Page of wands
21-23. Future liberation — ten of cups, seven of disks and six of cups

Hanged Man	Star	9W
6W	Tower	QD
PC		4S
Fool	Empress	Lovers
8W	KC	QC
	Justice	
Moon	KnS	10C
Sun	PW	7D
2S		6C

Or for the Astrological layout from page 144 of <u>The Tarot Reader</u>:

1. Jupiter
2. ten of swords
3. four of wands
4. ace of wands
5. five of swords
6. Judgement
7. Emperor
8. eight of swords
9. four of cups
10. Hermit
11. Juggler
12. Fool

                    Hermit

          Juggler   4C

     Fool   8S

  Jupiter   Emperor

        10S   Judgement

          4W   5S
                  AW

Or for the Elemental Spread from page
150 of <u>The Tarot Reader</u>:

1. Earth - ten of disks
2. Air - King of swords
3. Fire - Queen of wands
4. Water - ace of cups

   AC   QW   KS   10D

Or for the Chaktra Spread from page 152 of <u>The Tarot Reader</u>:

7. Crown - Universe
6. Third eye - two of wands
5. Throat - Emperor
4. Heart - two of cups
3. Solar plexus - Sun
2. Sex - Lovers
1. Root - Empress

Universe
2W
Emperor
2C
Sun
Lovers
Empress

Or for the As Above, So Below Spread found on page 156 of <u>The Tarot Reader</u>:

1-2. Behind - four of disks and seven of wands
3-4. Above - Juno and Jupiter
5-6. Before - three of cups and three of wands
7-8. Below - nine of disks and nine of wands
   9. You - Wheel

Juno   Jupiter

4D 7W   Wheel   3C 3W

9D   9W

Or for the Problem/Solution Spread found
on page 159 of <u>The Tarot Reader</u>:

1-4. Problem - five of swords, five of wands,
     eight of wands and Temperance
5-8. Action - two of swords, four of cups,
     Moon and three of disks
9-10. Lesson - Death and Strength

5S   5W   8W   Temperance
2S   4C   Moon   3D

Death   Strength

FURTHER IDEAS ABOUT
INTERPRETING A
TAROT READING

This section offers additional suggestions on how to prepare yourself for a reading and how to interpret the readings more clearly through close analysis of the spread in great detail. Before you read this section you may want to review pages 18 through 24 of <u>The Tarot</u>, entitled "Interpreting the Spread," which presents related information.

How to Approach a Reading

You must move toward the reading with an open mind and heart and a readiness to accept the truth without fear of change. Never read the cards if you feel incompetent or anxious. Give readings only when you feel confident and have complete faith in their ability to define the multi-layered activity of your life. If you sit down with your deck when you are afraid, depressed or in a negative mood, you will waste your time with the reading, as it will reflect your dark projections. As you should be calm and mellow before you read the cards, do whatever you must to reach a high wavelength where your senses are alert and ready to be aligned with the sacred source of ancient wisdom. Some card readers like to meditate, breathe deeply or pray before a reading in order to achieve a relaxed but heightened consciousness. The most powerful readings occur when you are energetic, inspired and at peace with yourself. The more positivity you bring to the reading the more intelligible, accurate and helpful it will be for you or the inquirer.

When you sit down to read, ask the deck specific questions and focus on receiving wisdom and guidance during the shuffling process so your interpretation will be crystal clear. Do not be intimidated by the pictures on the faces of the cards. Remember that <u>The Tarot</u> and <u>The Tarot Reader</u> are reference tools to lead you every step of the way through a reading. Keep an unflagging faith in the personal healing messages the Tarot reveals during a careful and enjoyable reading. The cards are user-friendly and not meant to be confusing, elusive or incomprehensible; they are designed to initiate discovery and increase your awareness. The Tarot is articulate to the point of eloquence once you know what the cards mean and how to utilize the deck in a reading. When you properly connect their visual attributes to their meaning and can translate what they symbolize in the people, events and circumstances of your life, you can give Tarot readings that can change the course of your destiny or bring to light the psychological and spiritual truths behind the drama of your existence.

Do not be fatalistic with a reading; look forward to the prospect of using the cards as a tool for finding out what is really going on behind the spectacle of reality. You will grow to love the Tarot as you receive uncanny, nearly miraculous readings that accurately describe what will come to pass.

Hazards of Speculation

One of the major dangers of card reading occurs when readers consciously or unconsciously project aspects of their own life into an interpretation they are giving to an inquirer. Inexperienced card readers sometimes make this error and should not read for the general public until they become more mature in their conduct and skillful with their deck. All card readers have to be careful not to make up information that is not directly related to the meaning of the cards as they fall in the spread positions. Unfortunately some readers invent material to tell the inquirer when their minds go blank during a reading, and they quickly think up something to say to fill the silence. These false interpretations make the reading nonsensical and destroy the positive spirit of the reading. If you encounter this problem, simply look up the definition of the card in <u>The Tarot</u> and <u>The Tarot Reader</u>, where you can always find the right words to describe any card as it applies to the particular spread you are examining.

Reading the Tarot requires intuition and imagination to unlock its system. Because the Tarot is inventive, you are constantly walking the thin line between fantasy and reality due to the enigmatic symbolism of the cards. Do not let yourself be manipulative or controlling when you give readings to other people, for that sort of behavior is not suitable in a Tarot reader. The goal of the Tarot is to expand your understanding of the cards through sincere, fulfilling readings that inspire you and satisfy your inquirers, who are helped by your accurate inside information.

How Often Should the Cards Be Read?

Another precarious situation arises when you read the cards too often. If you do too many readings, you may fail to correlate what comes to pass in your life with readings you have previously done and recorded in your journal. From time to time you should return to your journal and confirm your correct predictions for the future as well as your truthful assessment of the past and present. When you read too frequently, the power of the reading is diluted, and your ability to pick out the incidents, people and activities that the cards refer to gets muddled because you are flooding your mind with endless, pointless spreads. The Grand Cross uses eleven cards; add the four cards thrown for the Four Card Spread and you have 14 cards in 14 different positions, which should be more than enough to occupy your mind for one day. When you begin to read, you should try throwing the Grand Cross and Four Card spreads once a day as long as you maintain a balanced perspective on reality. Weekly try some of the other spreads found in The Tarot and The Tarot Reader such as the Three Card or As Above, So Below or Problem/ Solution spreads. More rarely utilize the Chaktra Spread and the Soulmate Search, and read the Astrological and Lifetimes spreads only once a year.

When you are new to the Tarot, it is helpful to read regularly if you can handle it and it does not interfere with your daily activities or blot out the more rational faculties of your intellect. You know you have overdone your readings when your interpretations get mixed up and your predictions become messy as you get confused about who or what the steady successions of pips, court cards and trumps stand for. If you repeatedly ask the same question of your deck, each new spread on the same subject defeats the austere clarity and poignancy that one single spread could offer you. Use repetitive spreads only when you are in control of your card-reading skills and need more information on a particularly prominent card or to expand on an aspect of a previous spread. The original reading is always easier to decipher and apply to the comings and goings of your life, because focusing on one or two spreads gives you just enough material to form a story. If in desperation you throw spread after spread, the truth of the reading will become so weak as to demoralize you and disappoint your inquirer. If you have done readings repeatedly, put your deck away and wait awhile before attempting another reading. Break your Tarot card routine and return to making completely conscious choices without the assistance of any divinatory tools. You need to reaffirm your self-reliance and let life pass by without the constant crutch of repeating Grand Cross Spreads over and over until neither the cards nor the spreads make sense. It is infinitely better to study the Tarot slowly and surely, using all three books in this Tarot trilogy, and to accumulate recorded readings in your journal. With a moderate number of readings given to yourself and others, this should help you master the

Tarot system.

You should never become totally dependent on the cards. Tarot readings should in no way rule your life; they can only give you a second unbiased, thought-provoking opinion with a universal perspective. The act of reading the cards forces you to sit down and think an issue over quietly in total concentration to arrive at an independent, enlightened solution to your problem. This is perhaps the most enriching aspect of the Tarot.

To run your life by the word of the cards is crazy, because eventually you could become too attached to reading them. People who are obsessed with the Tarot are usually obsessive about everything. Those who overidentify with the cards are often lacking in other areas of their lives. Too much fantasy, psychiatry or self-analysis is unbalancing to the body, mind and spirit, and as always the best approach is moderation.

If you become too serious about the cards, you should lighten up and have more fun with them. The deck is not meant to be grabbed in desperation but should be used on occasion when you have

a specific question and need to think things
over and get a glimpse of what is ahead
on your horizon.

How Long Does a Reading Take to Come True?

One of the most commonly asked questions
is when a reading will become reality.
Readings vary in how long they take to come
true. Often you find a reading lasts until
the next time you read on the same subject. Sometimes you receive a lifetime reading that totally examines the complete range
of what will happen to you as your destiny
unfolds. The cards most often symbolize
what you can expect to have happen until a
succeeding reading, though there are no set
boundaries around how long information
derived from a reading will apply to your
life. If you are doing the cards frequently,
this becomes extremely difficult to ascer-
tain because you are not giving the cards
enough time to come true. It is best not
to be so concerned with when events will
occur in the future; instead study the cards
and wait to see what materializes. Go
back to your Tarot journal where you have
faithfully recorded many of your most

astonishing and interesting readings and note the conspicuous cards that surfaced in the past when you chose to examine a certain issue.

If you insist on determining when a matter will happen in actuality, you need to look to the cards that fall in the future placements of a spread that will reflect what will occur later on. Cards in impending positions always seem strange, because what is yet to come is unknown at the time of the reading or has not been decided upon by the principal players represented by the court cards in the spread.

Sometimes readings do not make sense, but usually they are unbearably correct and informative as they give you the inside story on any subject you wish to explore. Some readings do not come true, and others are extremely difficult to interpret. This occurs when your mood is off or the cards are functioning at a level you cannot decipher at the time of the reading. One of the main purposes of your journal is to record these confusing readings so you can validate their significance at a later date.

Tarot readings fail when you are

reading for inquirers who are afraid of the cards because they have no knowledge of the Tarot and have been exposed to negative cartoon imagery of card readers. Some people are so undeveloped spiritually that they will not understand the language you use to explain their reading. This makes it even more impossible for you to give them a proper reading, and it is best to abandon the idea of doing the cards for such individuals unless you can handle criticism that could interrupt your careful synthesis of the spread and its components. The only solution to reading for a reluctant inquirer is to delineate the spread in the simplest terms.

Hints for Interpretation

When you begin to read the cards, you have a fixed notion of what each card symbolizes, courtesy of the definition sections of The Tarot and The Tarot Reader. Do not be put off because every card contains a handful of principal meanings. These different facets of the interpretation are not contradictory but complementary to each other. Each card has a traditional range of meanings that share a similar conceptual base because of the overall ideas and images associated with the card. As you read through the descriptive paragraphs that correspond to each of the 78 cards, you will connect the meaning of the card to the subject matter of the reading.

Once the cards are shuffled and dealt into the spread positions, you can create an interesting commentary on the entire picture of what the spread signifies. Look at the spread placement and blend it together with the definition of the card that lands there, which you can look up in The Tarot and The Tarot Reader. Eventually you will commit the cards' meanings to memory and rely on the books less and less when giving a reading.

If you have specific questions for your Tarot deck, you can omit the search for the significator through the subject piles. There is no need to pinpoint the area of your life the reading will explore because you are set on finding out more about a particular matter than getting an overall analysis of your entire existence. If you want a picture of the general forces that are influencing your reality, stick with the subject-combination step at the beginning of the reading, as described on pages 23 through 29 of The Tarot.

Tarot readings are lengthy explanations that provide details of the history of a matter. It is best to make your query as clear as possible. Decide ahead of time what you want to learn through the reading before you begin the shuffling process. Some sample questions you can pose to the Tarot deck are as follows:

What is going to happen to me regarding the area of my life defined by the subject-combination?

At what stage is my relationship with a certain individual?

Will I get the business deal?

Will I be successful with a particular project?

Should I go on this trip?

How can I make more money?

How can I find a more satisfying career?

What should I do to find my soulmate?

What is the best way to approach this person or situation?

What is this person thinking about me romantically?

If I move, will the location be right for me?

What is the spiritual lesson behind this situation?

If a card is surprisingly prominent when you throw the Grand Cross and Four Card spreads and you want to examine it further, go right into a brand-new Grand Cross after gathering up the Four Card Spread and reshuffle the entire deck while mentally asking who or what this particular card represents. The second Grand Cross will define what you can expect from the involvement of this card in the drama of your life.

It is easier to do consecutive spreads if the first one does not make sense or you posed a precise inquiry to the deck at the beginning of the reading. The Grand Cross is the best spread to use to try to clarify the message of the spread, but you could also try the Problem/Solution, Three Card and As Above, So Below layouts found in the spread section of <u>The Tarot Reader</u>.

Tarot cards move around in the time sequences of the spread positions, forming a logical pattern that reflects what is happening. If you do a Grand Cross on Monday and Jupiter is your outcome and by Thursday Jupiter surfaces as your self card, you can assume that what Jupiter symbolizes has gone from being a goal of yours to becoming part of your personality in how you approach the issue of the reading. Another example would be the King of wands as your first of the future Monday and by Thursday it is last of the present. In just a few days, you encountered the person or situation that the King of wands describes in both readings. Or the Tower appears for several weeks every time you do the cards and always in a future placement of the Grand Cross. Then suddenly a totally shocking truth is revealed to you at the same time that the Tower begins to show up in present tense positions of the spread. One day a woman can get the two of cups as her future environment even though at the time of the reading her life seems pretty loveless; but with the King of disks in her first of the future placement you can be sure of the type of man she should be on the lookout for.

Tarot cards can also disappear from your readings altogether, and you suddenly realize that, for example, the Emperor or the Empress has not been in your cards for months. When you finish interpreting any spread, glance over it and mentally tally how many swords, disks, cups, wands, court cards and trumps are present in its design. Also if the spread lacks a certain type of card, it would indicate that your life is deficient in that element. For example, no swords would signal that your intellectual functions are not being used to solve the situation that the reading

characterizes; no trumps would emphasize a lack of spiritual significance in the matter that the reading
examines.

TAROT CARDS IN PARTICULAR POSITIONS OF THE GRAND CROSS SPREAD

This section illustrates how to fine-tune the meaning of a card to fit a spread placement and offers many examples of adjusting the definition of a card to a position in the spread layout.

The Grand Cross is fully described on pages 34 through 38 of <u>The Tarot</u>. There you will find complete instructions for utilizing this Tarot spread in a reading. Here is a reminder of how to arrange the Grand Cross in its numerical order and design:

THE GRAND CROSS

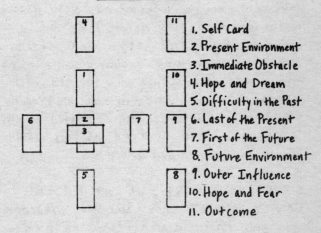

1. Self Card
2. Present Environment
3. Immediate Obstacle
4. Hope and Dream
5. Difficulty in the Past
6. Last of the Present
7. First of the Future
8. Future Environment
9. Outer Influence
10. Hope and Fear
11. Outcome

Swords

ACE OF SWORDS as your SELF CARD depicts you forging ahead with great determination and unification of purpose. Your mind is completely made up concerning the subject matter of the reading, and you know exactly how to proceed toward your goal or intention.

FIVE OF SWORDS as your IMMEDIATE OBSTACLE means you are taking the opinions of others either too seriously or not seriously enough, depending on the nature of the reading. Try not to let people get to you mentally, and keep a clear, steady mind even when those around you are losing theirs and distracting your focused intellectual energy. At the time of the reading you should avoid feeling defeated by any losses you have incurred, as this would block your forward progress.

SEVEN OF SWORDS as your FUTURE ENVIRONMENT shows you very much doing your own thing in an attempt to take advantage of your unique destiny. In the future you will become alienated from your social group. You will decide to break from your clique or colleagues and establish your own beliefs, thoughts, morality, general philosophy and pre-ferred life-style.

EIGHT OF SWORDS as your HOPE AND FEAR pictures you desperately trying to free yourself from some form of self-induced bondage. You are responsible for your helpless and powerless state, about which you complain to anyone who will listen. You secretly wish to extricate yourself from the emotional prison you have created, even though certain issues may be so painful that you cannot deal with them directly at this time. It is totally up to you whether you liberate yourself in the days to come; the card that surfaces in the outcome position of the spread indicates the likelihood of your making this release from what holds you back in your mind.

NINE OF SWORDS as your DIFFICULTY IN THE PAST states that you wanted something to happen very badly, but the matter did not turn out as you had hoped. Through this you have suffered pain due to the unkindness of others. You have emerged from a period of anxiety and despair and are ready to put it behind you. This time of testing will serve you in the future, as you are now hardened toward hatred, criticism and bad treatment directed at you by unhappy people.

QUEEN OF SWORDS as your LAST OF THE PRESENT characterizes your headstrong quality as well as your intellectual ability. As the Queen of swords you communicated endlessly in an effort to push through the plan you were working on, which necessitated this particular behavior. As this card is leaving your life, this unemotional behavior is no longer required of you. You have said all you have to say on the subject matter of the reading, and your reign of severity has come to an end.

Disks

ACE OF DISKS as your SELF CARD shows you having a definite gift or talent that could blossom, given time, creative assistance or even material support in the form of financial aid, an opportunity to learn, or a chance to get involved in a new field of interest where you would have great potential for success. As your self card, the ace of disks implies that you must develop any abilities that lie dormant inside you, waiting to be put to use.

FOUR OF DISKS as your IMMEDIATE OBSTACLE describes how you want to know exactly what you own in order to establish some genuine permanent security for yourself. Whether or not you are content with what you have gained thus far, your need to accumulate possessions is somehow blocking your progress right now. Also, the four of disks as an obstacle would stress the trouble you are having supporting yourself financially. This card helps you get in touch with your own personal power and gives you a chance to prove yourself wherever it lands in the spread.

SIX OF DISKS as your HOPE AND DREAM

would reveal that you want to establish a creative or monetary partnership with another that involves a complementary exchange of assets or talents in order to get ahead in your chosen field. If this disk represents a love relationship, it describes two people who have much to give each other materially. This union will grow into a practical and workable balanced arrangement.

EIGHT OF DISKS as your LAST OF THE PRESENT specifies that you have just finished a project you have worked on long and hard to produce the best possible results. You took full responsibility for completing the tasks that were handed to you so you could undergo an apprenticeship and master a valuable skill or area of talent through your efforts.

PAGE OF DISKS as your OUTCOME shows that you will eventually play the role of the serviceable, helpful, detail-oriented, hardworking Page of disks. You may ultimately end up in a position where you have to deal with documents, literature, contracts or getting information down in writing. You may become one who will keep track of financial records as an assistant to a King of disks in the world of commerce, where he will train you to handle all aspects of a certain operation.

Cups

FOUR OF CUPS as your PRESENT ENVIRON-MENT means that at the time of the reading you are not taking action on any emotional issues. Instead you are waiting out a period of feeling distant and distracted from the person you are currently involved with. You remain in an unhappy situation that can be relieved only when someone or something better comes along to give you the initiative to break the already weak tie. You are in a fog about ending the alliance and disgusted at having to continue the masquerade with a person you do not love. As the influence of the four of cups leaves your life, you will be more stable and know exactly what sort of relationship you want next.

SIX OF CUPS as your PRESENT ENVIRON-

MENT implies that you are extending your social circle in an effort to increase your personal happiness. You are trying to give more of yourself in all your encounters with others by expressing your feelings more openly and readily. You are going to great lengths to meet positive, loving people outside your usual environments and are experiencing a rebirth of emotion for those you reside with or already know through your daily activities.

SEVEN OF CUPS as your PRESENT ENVIRONMENT illustrates that you are making a choice between fantasy and reality right now. It also implies an increase in your imaginative faculties and shows you dreaming quite intensely about all the wonderful things you want to accomplish in the future. Though many of your visions will come true, some are figments of your own invention and will never be actualized.

NINE OF CUPS as your FIRST OF THE FUTURE depicts how emotionally satisfied you will become shortly. This card lets you know that permanent happiness is close at hand. You should prepare yourself for all the good things to come in the days ahead, things that will make you more blissfully content than ever before.

KNIGHT OF CUPS as your OUTCOME adds a question mark to the end of the reading. It is hard to interpret exactly how this Knight will manifest himself, because of his generally elusive nature. As your outcome, this card indicates that you will receive an offer you will welcome, but there will be a twist to the true value of what could come your way through the Knight of Cups character. The matter the reading examines will turn out differently than you expect, and you should be extra discriminating toward the person to whom you must say either yes or no.

KING OF CUPS as your OUTER INFLUENCE refers to a male authority figure who will become very prominent in the days ahead. He may represent a business deal pending between you and an equally matched intense and intriguing person. In love this card would symbolize someone you feel terribly attracted to in a hopeless way. The person this card indicates will add spice to your existence and could become the single most important individual to you later on.

Wands

ACE OF WANDS as your DIFFICULTY IN THE PAST shows the trouble you have had as you attempt to start over again in life. Somehow through sheer willpower you have struggled to recharge your batteries with an exhilarating surge of fresh energy. You are completely ready to develop yourself by taking creative action in the future. You are fully prepared to strike out in new directions, and this is highly beneficial to your ultimate success.

SIX OF WANDS as your SELF CARD implies that you have the capacity to achieve great things. At the time of the reading you are waging a fight to win a particular battle. This entanglement requires an indefatigable spirit to defeat any negativity that could block you from reaching your goal. This six implies that your will is in accordance with your actions as you strive for a passionately fulfilling life.

EIGHT OF WANDS as your PRESENT ENVIRONMENT describes you pulling together many loose ends within a short period of time concurrent with the reading. You are experiencing an urgency that makes you move as fast as you can in the areas the reading defines. In terms of love, the eight of wands could depict you being overwhelmed by impulsive, almost obsessive feelings for one individual.

QUEEN OF WANDS as your DIFFICULTY IN THE PAST reveals that you have been strong, demanding and relentless, especially in how you treat those around you, in order to establish yourself creatively. Due to the control you have over the situation the reading examines, you can go forth in the future and develop your social and artistic skills. The Queen of wands can also represent another person who would have had a similar influence over you in the past and because of that previous role will be a support to you in the coming days.

KING OF WANDS as your LAST OF THE

PRESENT indicates that a prominent individual who has been a true friend to you is
leaving your life. Even if he remains a
part of your world, his power over you
is on the wane. This King can symbolize
a person who has been very good to you
or has done you a righteous favor. In love
he could stand for someone you cared for
who is fading quickly into the past. As
the King of wands is crystal clear in
his intentions, you were always certain
of the exact nature of his feelings for
you. It is best to regard the King of
wands as a kindly man you came together
with to experience supportive, mutual
and perhaps platonic love. The time
has now come to part and go your separate ways, continuing to hold each other
in high esteem.

Trumps

THE FOOL as your FIRST OF THE
FUTURE means there will soon be
sudden changes and surprises in the
area of your life the reading explores.
Expect the unexpected and be aware
of everyone and everything in your orbit

in the days to come, for these people and things will bear a forceful transformation for you. You will feel carefree and foolish in terms of the subject of the spread and will not take responsibility for your involvement with others.

THE JUGGLER as your OUTER INFLUENCE shows that someone will be willful and self-centered and his behavior will directly affect the forecast of things to come. He may be so secretive that you remain in the dark about his true character or intentions. The Juggler can also stand for an individual you worship from afar due to his or her reputation, charisma or public image, whom you may not personally know. Or this trump could indicate that you are acting in the manner of the Juggler toward those around you.

JUPITER as your DIFFICULTY IN THE PAST demonstrates that you have been through the experience of spiritual initiation, which you can now use to serve others through teaching or healing. You have remained a devoted, evolving person, no matter what the hardships, and have come to the point of being your own judge, mentor and guide as you now make all your own decisions. Your metaphysical interests, which have met with opposition in the past, will be your strength in the time ahead.

THE CHARIOT as your HOPE AND DREAM says you want to go on a trip or follow a particular predestined path, especially if the reading was thrown to analyze a potential journey. The twist here is that your traveling companion will be a fateful surprise to you, or you may end up taking off by yourself when you thought you were going with another or a group. Due to the exalted position of this trump in the Grand Cross, you are being told that your ultimate dreams will come true no matter what. You are moving toward fulfilling them at precisely the correct pace for the purpose of your spiritual education.

THE HERMIT as your IMMEDIATE OBSTACLE describes your high standards,

which often lead you to seek out solitude
for making the right decisions and producing perfect work. You need silence to
attain total concentration and master
your awareness of what the reading examines. Your growing knowledge combined
with your desire for independence does
not make life easy right now, but eventually you will figure out how to share your
wisdom with others so they can benefit
from this aspect of your personality.

STRENGTH as your SELF CARD emphasizes the unflagging courageous spirit
that you have adopted in order to keep
yourself healthy, strong and prepared
to take on any challenges that cross your
path. This trump implies that your natural energy and talent are poised and
ready to lead you to success as long as
you stay clear and clean and balanced
and continue to discipline yourself to be
a powerfully productive force in your
environment.

THE UNIVERSE as your FIRST OF
THE FUTURE reveals just how complicated
and extensive your plans will become so

you can actualize the purpose of your current incarnation and follow your preordained destiny with an ever-evolving enlightenment. Your ultimate accomplishments will be much greater than you think, so be patient while in steady pursuit of your true purpose. Make yourself number one in the future and do not let anyone or anything pull you away from the direction that your soul most desires to pursue. On a different note, the Universe or the World card could signal that you will be involved in a worldwide or international exchange that will be dedicated to saving the planet itself.

SEVEN TAROT READINGS

Reading One

This reading was given to a female artist who has the Queen of disks as her significator. She was particularly interested in receiving information concerning a recent encounter with a male art-gallery owner who seemed eager to represent her artwork. During their initial meeting they connected really well, but she sensed he was attracted to her romantically. She wanted the reading to make her more aware of what was going on between them and whether anything would come about professionally from this individual. The subject-combination of the reading was WORK AND BUSINESS and MONEY AND MATERIAL MATTERS.

THE GRAND CROSS

Your SELF CARD is the QUEEN OF WANDS, who depicts you as a champion of your own interests by coming on strong and exuding confidence whenever you can and wherever you go. As your self card, she shows you feeling courageous about expressing your creative and passionate natures. You are eager to interact with others to advance yourself artistically as you know they could inspire you to become more productive in your output as an artist. This particular gallery owner is just one avenue to investigate for marketing your work. You are smart and enthusiastic; he perceives this and is encouraged by your obvious dedication to accomplishing your career goals.

Your PRESENT ENVIRONMENT is the ACE OF CUPS, which reaffirms that purely emotional energy was exchanged between you and the gallery owner on a real heart level. You both genuinely and spontaneously liked each other and thoroughly enjoyed communicating on a similar wavelength. Because you are functioning as the Queen of wands, you are sending out vibrations that naturally invite love into your life. By being more open and receptive toward others, you draw their attention to your charm and sunny countenance. This ace shows that meeting this person has inspired you to become more actively involved in getting your career together, as the time and attention he gave you boosted your self-confidence.

Your IMMEDIATE OBSTACLE is JUPITER, which indicates how much you have already learned from this experience and how crossing the path of this man has been a major lesson for you. You might become involved with him in a business venture, but this trump as your obstacle suggests the difficulty you could have trying to join his group of colleagues. There may be insurmountable problems due to your spiritual philosophy and Queen of wands personality adding force and honesty to the way you approach people.

Your HOPE AND DREAM is the NINE OF WANDS, which specifies that your first priority should be keeping yourself on top of matters to protect your dearest dreams and most cherished desires. As the Queen of wands, it is in your best interest to maintain a dominant position and not let anyone or anything threaten your basic security. This wand may bring a slight delay in attaining your greatest ambitions in life due to its placement in the spread, but you must never give up the struggle to establish yourself as an artist.

Your DIFFICULTY IN THE PAST is THE MOON, which depicts the overwhelming and bewildering feelings you have had about the issue of the reading. You have been uncertain about how to sell your artwork and how to deal with particular people and situations in your quest for success. Perhaps you were shaky emotionally in the past when faced with the task of self-promotion or were under the influence of mood-altering substances that clouded your mind and actions. This period is now coming to a close, and the ordeal has made you stronger, so in the future you will have more wisdom and visual imagery at your disposal to apply to your creative work. The Moon gives you lots of ideas and material that you should share with others who need your knowledge to improve the conditions of their lives (Jupiter as your obstacle). This trump can also symbolize the years you have spent trying to succeed in a Neptunian industry such as the art world.

Your LAST OF THE PRESENT is the NINE OF DISKS, which specifies that you are already capable of producing marketable art that could generate a nice income for you if sold through the right agent or gallery. Your talent has reached a point of development where your skills and inspiration are so reliable that you may even take them for granted later on. With the nine of wands held high as your hope and dream and the Moon behind you in the past, you have many poignant experiences to draw from. Your muddled or failed attempts at selling your work unfortunately preceded the actual maturation of your artistic abilities, though this position of the nine of disks shows that your genius has been recognized by others to some degree already.

Your FIRST OF THE FUTURE is the KNIGHT OF DISKS, and your FUTURE ENVIRONMENT is the QUEEN OF DISKS. The man in question will come through for you and make things happen for your career. These two disk court cards say that you could earn money together for sure. He will be solid, honest, supportive and serviceable, and you will want to put your life in his hands. The Queen of disks is also your significator and represents you rising to meet the Knight of disks halfway. You would make good use of time spent working on common projects should you ultimately decide to take up his material offer. Your relationship with him has brought out the Queen of wands in you, and with the Queen of disks in your future you can handle the financial realities that accompany selling the pieces you produce. You will have to be practical about your expenditures if you want to pull your career together, and you should showcase your fully developed nine of disks abilities in their best light. The Knight of disks is always helpful to the extreme and is a wonderful team player. He could become the cornerstone of the foundation of your artistic destiny. You will definitely talk to him or see him again, and both your cards and his will be laid on the table, so to speak. The final positions of this spread and the Four Card Spread that follows will point out what will happen between you and him in the end.

Your OUTER INFLUENCE is THE CHARIOT, which tells you it is just a matter of time until the puzzle pieces of your life fit together. By and by, everyone and everything around you will help you move as fast as possible toward your proper destination artistically. You should relax and accept any uncomfortable situations you have to endure due to the involvement of other people in your business affairs by realizing that you are experiencing exactly what you need to go through for purposes of your spiritual education.

Your HOPE AND FEAR is THE STAR, which means you will resist certain imminent opportunities that could give you a chance to be noticed or placed in the spotlight, even though up to the time of the reading you have had trouble getting any recognition at all. Part of you wants to shine at center stage, but another part of you holds back due to fear of speaking, leading, teaching or making a total commitment to a cause through your work as an artist.

Your OUTCOME is the KNIGHT OF

CUPS, who indicates a definite offer coming from the Knight of disks, but there will be something questionable about the deal. The Knight of cups, ace of cups and Queen of wands all affirm that he is attracted to you and is considering making some sort of proposition to you that may be inappropriate. The Star in the hope and fear placement emphasizes your concern about what you might have to do to enhance your career. The Knight of cups unfortunately has an unstable personality that often leads him to extend empty or unsuitable overtures.

THE FOUR CARD SPREAD

WORK AND BUSINESS is THE LOVERS, which reiterates the fact that your connection to the gallery owner could be potentially complex, as there is a genuine affinity between the two of you. This trump falls in the position that is the key to what will come to pass if you work together. Before you do anything, you must decide if you are going to accept his advances. His turning up as the Knight

of disks as well means that his offer
of assistance has a lot to do with your
appealing to him in more than a business sense.

LOVE AND PARTNERSHIP is the
QUEEN OF SWORDS, showing the
likelihood that you are interested in him
only intellectually. Though you came on
like the Queen of wands, in the end
you will act cold and distant, which
could lead him to withdraw his interest
in you, as he could be more fascinated by
the woman in you than the artist in you.
This card suggests you saying no to his
Knight of cups offer, which would end any
discussion of working together.

TROUBLE AND CONFLICT is the
EIGHT OF WANDS, which implies that
this matter will be brought up rather
quickly between you and settled one
way or another equally soon. He urgently
wants to express his feelings and will come
on a little too strong and fast in terms
of what he proposes to you as the Knight
of cups. The Chariot and the Star from
the Grand Cross Spread demonstrate

how attaining recognition is crucial to your career, but you may forgo this chance for success and ultimately decide to reject his invitation forcefully (Queen of Swords in the love placement).

MONEY AND MATERIAL MATTERS is the TWO OF WANDS, which depicts your lonely struggle to establish yourself and make some money in your chosen field. You should continue to be pushy and willful in your quest for attention even though you are unenthusiastic about being in the light of the Star that singles you out for your work. This gallery owner is just one of many you will encounter as you take control of your material affairs by representing yourself in business. In the end, he may be a temporary catalyst whose role is to move you forward in your attempt to gain monetarily through your art. It does not seem likely that he will help you unless you accept his terms in the very near future.

Reading Two

This reading was given to a female author

who has the Queen of disks as her significator.
She wanted to know whether she would be
hired for a teaching position at a nearby
college for which she had been inter-
viewed prior to the reading. The subject-
combination of the reading was WORK
AND BUSINESS and MONEY AND MATERIAL
MATTERS.

THE GRAND CROSS

Your SELF CARD is THE SUN, which indicates that you are going into this experience with your eyes, mind and heart wide
open. You know you have a lot to give and
are aware how valuable this job could be
for you and for the students as well. You
have much warmth, positivity and aliveness
to spread to those who could flourish from
contact with you. When you walked in the
door for your interview, you were like fresh
air and sunlight. You naturally raise the
consciousness of others, especially those who
are eager to learn. Your personality helps
your garden to grow in the work and money
arena, which this spread will explore.

Your PRESENT ENVIRONMENT is

JUPITER, which says you currently have a great deal of wisdom about the subjects you would teach should you become a professor. You know many secrets concerning your interests and have an understanding of these subjects in a historical sense. You love to study and you take ideas, books and education seriously. With the Sun as your self card and a subject-combination of work and money, it seems as though you are ripe and ready to guide those who could benefit from your influence as a caring authority who would gently steer them in the right direction.

Your IMMEDIATE OBSTACLE is the KNIGHT OF CUPS. This indicates that a definite offer of employment will come from the school, but it will not be what you want or expect. There may be loopholes in vague promises no one plans to live up to in the end. It seems your prospective employers have already decided to give you the job, but you feel insecure about joining the faculty, or perhaps you have an inkling that the institution itself is unstable. These could be some of the factors that make you fluctuate about taking the position. You can be sure that one or more of the oral commitments made to you will not hold up in reality, especially when it comes time to be paid. This Knight emphasizes that the administrators want to hire you as a teacher, but they are uncertain about how to handle you for some reason.

Your HOPE AND DREAM is the HANGED MAN, which shows that you are ready to sacrifice everything to fulfill your dream of doing service to humanity through your ultimate career choice. The presence of Jupiter reiterates that you want to uphold the highest, most absolute principles, and to do this you must leave behind people and habits that do not honor your ideals. A total change of direction is under way in the area of your long-term goals. You are prepared to dedicate yourself to searching for work that will support your spiritual development. Due to this tendency, you will decline potential employment that seems dead end, frivolous, materialistic or uninteresting.

Your DIFFICULTY IN THE PAST is the FOUR OF SWORDS, which indicates that you have been cloistered prior to the reading and that you have gained much strength from your separateness, which is also a result of Jupiter as your present environment. By distancing yourself and staying silent, you have obtained peace of mind, which will be a plus to you in the future. The sort of nonattachment that accompanies the four of swords, the Hanged Man and Jupiter has prepared you to deal with what lies ahead.

Your LAST OF THE PRESENT is THE EMPEROR, which pictures you being totally in control, knowing what you want and taking all necessary precautionary organizational steps toward securing your little empire in the work and money fields. This trump states that you have shown yourself to be more than capable for this job. Should you accept it you would be responsible, thorough and dependable to the extreme. The Emperor can also symbolize you or another growing more mature, worldly and sophisticated.

Your FIRST OF THE FUTURE is THE MOON, which says you will see the dark side of the situation and be bewildered and confused by what comes to pass should you accept the appointment. Be on the lookout for the use of illusion or downright lying by the school. Be crystal clear about the particulars of the teaching position and leave no questions unasked regarding the situation. The Moon tells you there will be some delay. The school could wait for a while before making an offer to you, so be alert to this sort of behavior.

Your FUTURE ENVIRONMENT is the NINE OF SWORDS, which makes it likely that you will agonize over this matter and become unpleasantly preoccupied by thoughts of the enormous amount of work that would be required should you accept the post. This new burden could disrupt your life and distract you by taking time and attention away from your writing. Also, the nine of swords heralds a forecast that you should let the unkindness of those at the college roll off your back and not take it to heart. Do not feel any personal loss or dejection due to the brusque conduct of the school officials. This sword does not bode well for how the school would treat you should you join its staff. All close-knit working environments breed gossip and backstabbing if people are present who poison and disorganize the smooth flow of daily business.

Your OUTER INFLUENCE is the QUEEN OF CUPS, which symbolizes that you will not confront the administrators as much as you should and will just let things unfold naturally or gradually. If the Queen of cups represents someone else, his or her free-form behavior will severely affect your future involvement with this college. If there are no prominent females influencing this situation, this card suggests not making any unnecessary demands on anyone regarding this matter. This Queen also characterizes others being attracted to you — especially in conjunction with the Sun — or it can mean that the offer from the college will come to you through a magnetic, mysterious woman whom you may or may not already know.

Your HOPE AND FEAR is the THREE OF DISKS, which makes it likely that you will hesitate about completing the job and may want to leave halfway through the semester. You would not enjoy the tremendous amount of work the position would require of you. This could lead to thoughts of quitting after you have begun to teach, or accepting the appointment may be questionable with the Knight of Cups as your obstacle. In the end you could find yourself sitting on a fence about becoming a professor because with the three of disks you have a heavy work load from other occupations.

Your OUTCOME is the PAGE OF SWORDS, which always indicates that phone calls will be made back and forth until a decision is arrived at or a deal is struck. It can show you checking out the situation by gathering inside information over the telephone and trying to get the inside story on the school.

Beware of trickery in the days to come, especially with the Moon as your first of the future. Crucial details may be hidden from you to give the school the upper hand in contractual negotiations. This Page can also be interpreted as the actual call you will receive offering the job to you. The three of disks as your hope and fear questions whether you will accept the position and how long you would stick it out if you did accept it.

THE FOUR CARD SPREAD

WORK AND BUSINESS is JUNO, which implies that your intuition will be clear and reliable and you will understand the spiritual reasons behind your work situation. You know by instinct that this teaching assignment would help you develop skills that you could use later on. Trust your spontaneous insights into this matter, for they are correct. Any presentiments about your career picture are accurate and should be taken seriously. This trump also points out that you could wing it during your lectures without much preparation in advance. Your inner wisdom will rise up from your memory-laden subconscious and pour forth from your mouth as you speak to the class.

LOVE AND PARTNERSHIP is the QUEEN OF DISKS, which describes you as a practical person who takes on any work that comes your way in an effort to add to the collective wealth of your relationships. You consider your associations with others purely in terms of the material status they could afford you. This job would ease any financial problems you share with your mate, close friends or colleagues and would help you increase your self-worth tremendously. You are reliable and supportive to everyone with whom you work, and with the Emperor as your last of the present, you are totally prepared for the added responsibility of another occupation.

TROUBLE AND CONFLICT is the FOUR OF DISKS, which emphasizes that you will continue to strive to achieve economic security. More than anything, you must be certain you have enough to live on, but you are finding it difficult to obtain a solid money base. This is perhaps the main reason you applied for this position in the first place: to make a little extra on the side. The three of disks as your hope and fear in conjunction with the four shows the deep concerns you have about your budget. The Queen of disks in your love placement implies that your employment picture is directly related to your alliances with others.

MONEY AND MATERIAL MATTERS is the TEN OF WANDS, which depicts how your pursuit of stability affects many areas of your life. You are overburdened by work as it is and would find it impossible to take a breather once classes started. Other business interests of yours stack up tasks for you to complete, and these additional commitments must be honored. You will need every ounce of energy and more to fulfill the demands made on you, so get plenty of rest and take care of yourself and you will not get run down in the months ahead.

Reading Three

This reading was given to a male who has the King of Cups as his significator and who wanted to know about his career outlook. He held a routine office job that enabled him to save money, but he was experiencing no real satisfaction from his current situation. He was confused about his general direction in life, though he eventually wanted to find a more creative occupation. The subject-combination of the reading was double WORK AND BUSINESS.

THE GRAND CROSS

Your SELF CARD is JUDGEMENT, which is a heavy trump to begin the spread. It implies that you are making major decisions right now and are looking at life with greater seriousness than ever before. You may be acting overly critical toward others or demanding too much from everyone around you. This trump as your self card is a sign that your personality is being eclipsed by the qualities associated with Judgement.

Your PRESENT ENVIRONMENT is the KING OF SWORDS, an authoritative, intellectual, unemotional man who is unpleasant but teaches you a tremendous amount of knowledge that can be applied to your work. He is helping you develop your brain power and plays an influential role at a time when you are at the crossroads of your destiny due to Judgement. This King could also represent you acting cold and detached toward others because you are totally absorbed in your own thoughts and concerns that revolve around your desire to drastically change the course of your existence.

Your OBSTACLE is THE SUN, which shows the problems you are having because you are becoming aware that you should follow a direction that would make you more content and cheerful. You may presently be moving to a warmer, more southerly location or to a new and happier place where you could enjoy a higher standard of living. You might be considering a short trip to an area of intense heat or sunlight, which is the right atmosphere for thinking over the important and imposing decisions facing you now (Judgement). Often the Sun in this position represents the summer season as an obstacle for you.

Your HOPE AND DREAM is the SEVEN OF SWORDS, which in this Grand Cross placement explains that you should strive to be your own person. You need to make your own choices and create your own status quo if you are to succeed in a big way. You must live by your own rules in order to fulfill your lifetime potential. Following your individual philosophy will lead to greater joy and freedom and will bring into reach the dreams you hold dear.

Your DIFFICULTY IN THE PAST is the PAGE OF DISKS, which says that you have already done your homework and completed your apprenticeship. Perhaps you were forced to learn how to handle assignments that will be required by the area of business you enter in the future. The seven and the King of swords symbolize that you will probably have your own commercial concern eventually, but first you must undergo training supervised by a tough King of swords mentor who challenges you to work hard. All of your jobs down the road will demand that you function in a clerical manner, whether your tool be pen, paper, file or computer.

Your LAST OF THE PRESENT is the TWO OF WANDS, which indicates that recently you have been trying to establish your career by yourself and without assistance from anyone else. You have initiated all that has come to pass in terms of the subject matter of the reading. Nobody has really helped you thus far, and your only true success has come from positions you found for yourself while actively seeking employment. Due to your intense desire to do well and get somewhere, you have channeled all your energy into taking control of your job picture. Your will is totally directed toward expressing your creativity through outer world endeavors, but achieving this goal has been difficult up to this point.

Your FIRST OF THE FUTURE is THE HERMIT, which implies that you will take an inner journey in the future. You will get deeply involved in searching for the truth inside yourself and spending time in thought and reflection. You will become more self-reliant and stop using others to fill a gap in your life or help you out of a jam. The Hermit in a reading completely focused on work screams out self-employment, so this theme is repeated again. You must become more independent and perhaps branch out on your own in the coming days. This seems certain with the seven of swords as your hope and dream.

Your FUTURE ENVIRONMENT is the KNIGHT OF SWORDS, which shows you harbor some insecurity about your ability to make things happen for yourself. You may be too persistent, overpowering or condescending as an overreaction to your own sense of inadequacy. You are especially irritating and illogically severe with your colleagues at work, whom you may be ignoring as you race around in a rash, self-centered manner.

You may be too immature intellectually to handle what lies ahead for you, and emotionally you must become more relaxed, confident and generous with others.

Your OUTER INFLUENCE is the FOUR OF WANDS, which illustrates rewards coming to you for your intense effort on the job as typified by the two of wands. You will begin to experience more passionate contentment, especially in your home environment. You will be more comfortable with letting people share your world. You need to find a collective atmosphere where you could be happy and feel as if you belong. You are going to require the support of others in the future when you will implement the decisions you are making now concerning work. Down the road you will become more friendly and more of a team player to counterbalance your tendency to be driven like the King and Knight of swords. You must learn how to pleasantly combine business and camaraderie by forging a sense of community with those you collaborate with all day long.

Your HOPE AND FEAR is the TWO OF CUPS, which tells you that the true intimacy of a monogamous relationship is something you will seek in the time ahead even though opening up your heart to another scares you. This card depicts a mutual exchange of emotions and compassion between two people, which reflects refined, dignified and honorable values. This cup in conjunction with the four of wands says that your ability to get along with others will be on trial later when you will have to show the utmost respect to those you choose to love.

Your OUTCOME is the THREE OF DISKS, which represents completion of a project or finishing up a particular job. In a broader sense, it shows you eventually settling in a field of interest or a position that is permanent. This card symbolizes that one or more of four things will happen: you will use two or three of your most prominent talents in your ultimate choice of occupation; you may start your own business; you could end up having a few different operations going at once.; or you could find a couple of practical people to be partners with in your endeavors. This outcome implies that you will always be employed and busy working to implement your most useful ideas.

THE FOUR CARD SPREAD

WORK AND BUSINESS is the PAGE OF SWORDS, a messenger of information whose role is to check things out on the sly like a spy. This card could indicate that you are being watched and examined by your boss or co-workers or that you are caught in a web of gossip with them. This Page also stresses speaking, talking with the public, being on the telephone and communicating on the job. Alternately this card can be interpreted as you peeking out from behind a curtain to gather inside details and background intelligence at your place of employment. In the highest sense, the Page of swords links you to your subconscious mind through meditation or instantaneous telepathic ability and gives you a crystal clear mind. This

sword Page reveals that one of your
secret plans is to find some privacy so
you can map out schemes and agendas
that you can later actualize. As this
card falls in the work placement, which
is the total focus of the reading, acting
like the Page of swords is crucial to
your career success.

LOVE AND PARTNERSHIP is the
THREE OF CUPS, which tells you to enjoy
mixing with others socially, as this makes
you happy and satisfies your emotional
needs for the time being. With the two
of cups as your hope and fear, this three
is a clear indication that you use this
empty type of socialization to avoid
meaningful connections because you are
afraid of true communion with another.
You prefer your relationships to be
casual and temporary, and you choose
to mingle in crowds rather than go out
with one person in particular. As the
Hermit, you enjoy the anonymity, but
with the three of cups, you do not
want the responsibility of involvement,
and your only desire is to be in among
people who are having a good time together.

TROUBLE AND CONFLICT is the ACE OF DISKS, which announces the arrival of money, talent and possessions, but as a difficulty due to the spread position where the ace has surfaced. You may be having problems developing your abilities, building up some financial reserve or stockpiling practical expertise that you could use to master the material world. This ace describes you as being surrounded by gifted, active people who can aid you in your quest for success as you start out on your career path. Allow others to teach you what they know, as there is infinite value to be derived from their experience. This will help you establish yourself in your own business or form a partnership with others later on. This ace can also speak of starting over monetarily and the challenges associated with such a harrowing task.

MONEY AND MATERIAL MATTERS is the FOUR OF SWORDS, which implies that you have been thinking a lot about what you are going to do while Judgement is an intrinsic part of your personality and the Hermit looms before you in the immediate future. Being apart from others in solitude is somehow tied to your financial condition. If nothing is really happening work-wise, just wait out this slow and quiet period with great patience and do not take any hasty action. Instead give an endless amount of thought to choosing your employment direction, which has been overshadowed by the Page of disks in the past. Something concrete always emerges from the calm of the four of swords as it prepares you to take control of your career down to the last detail.

Reading Four

This reading was given to a male who has the King of cups as his significator. He requested information about his love life, as he was single and greatly feeling the need for a girlfriend. Also, he wanted to know whether he should leave his current job for something new and when he should initiate the move. The subject-combination of the reading was MONEY AND MATERIAL MATTERS and LOVE AND PARTNERSHIP.

THE GRAND CROSS

Your SELF CARD is the SEVEN OF SWORDS, which portrays you going your own way right now and trying to establish your unique identity in order to recapture your individual freedom. Your personal philosophy is defeating collective reality, and you are very relieved to be able to be yourself. This sword describes your get-lost attitude toward society at large, and you long to be released from what others force upon you, which you find intolerable and suffocating to your spirit. This sword shows you getting stronger and more sure of yourself intellectually as you stand up to be counted and speak your mind without fear of retaliation.

Your PRESENT ENVIRONMENT is the TWO OF SWORDS, which stresses the importance of utilizing blind faith to get through a period of sitting and waiting patiently, which is the opposite of the requirement of the previous card. You need to remain confident and maintain a positive attitude toward your future while concentrating totally on what you

want in the days ahead. Having to bide
your time is frustrating because the seven
of swords characterizes you as itching
to get going. The two of swords tells you
that ultimately you will express your
individuality and be accepted for who you
are, but do not expect any miracles
overnight.

Your IMMEDIATE OBSTACLE is the
ACE OF SWORDS, which indicates that
while you sweat out the interval of the
two of swords, you must make a decision
that champions your own interests
and allows you to go your own way (seven
of swords). The first three cards in this
spread depict all your thoughts and com-
munications in terms of money and love
presently. The ace, two and seven of
swords symbolize that you are striving
to make a firm commitment to establish
your own identity. Your attitude may
seem slightly foolish because your current situation does not reflect your true
potential (two of swords). You derive
pleasure from the fact that you do not
fit into any neat group or category (seven
of swords). Therefore you seek to discover

who or what is really right for you by experimenting with all your ideas about life. Once you choose your unique plan you can silently and diligently devote all your energy toward developing the skill, career or activity you select in the end.

Your HOPE AND DREAM is the KING OF WANDS. This is a dominant but kind male figure whom you admire, or he may stand for this facet of your own personality. This King is good, honest, helpful and totally supportive of the goals of others. He can symbolize someone who comes to your aid in an honorable fashion and energetically assists you, though you may want more from him than he can give you. The King of wands in this particular position of the Grand Cross emphasizes that this person or aspect of your character is central to the ultimate outcome of this reading.

Your DIFFICULTY IN THE PAST is the EIGHT OF DISKS, which describes how hard it has been to commit yourself to learning a craft that you are naturally good at and secretly wish to perfect to an art. In the past you avoided accepting any apprenticeship that could further you creatively, but now you are really ready to get to work for the first time. If you have been toiling your whole life, this card would suggest that you labored against your will, and this caused you difficulties; but in the future, your dedication to your career will be your greatest ally and strength.

Your LAST OF THE PRESENT is the KING OF SWORDS, symbolizing an authority figure who is leaving your existence and will no longer be judging your every move. If you are this King, this placement would be saying you can ease up on ruling by the sword because of your increased self-assurance and the faith you have developed in the value of your own thoughts (two of swords). The decision you must make (ace of swords) will help you relax about standing apart from the crowd due to your ideas (seven of swords). These ideas should be used to your advantage as the powerful King of swords.

Your FIRST OF THE FUTURE is the KING OF DISKS, who represents you getting to work even more intensely than the eight. This King can also identify someone who has access to wealth or business connections who will be looking for an assistant with the particular abilities you felt compelled to develop in the past whether you wanted to or not (eight of disks). If the King of disks refers to a person you will work for, he will aid in nurturing your natural talent. Through your involvement with him, you will be handling more money than ever before, so be ready to be more financially responsible when this opportunity comes your way. This change in your material situation could come through your own efforts but is more likely to happen due to someone who fits the description of either the King of swords, King of wands or King of disks, as you have three strong male personalities floating around this spread so far. Kings express masculine energy in a prominent manner. In your daily encounters, try to figure out who these Kings may be in your life. If you find yourself behaving in their archetypal way, try to cultivate the nicest aspects of their conduct.

Your FUTURE ENVIRONMENT is the TEN OF DISKS, which announces a buildup of monetary security as a result of your knack for business based on genius you have inherited genetically through your family, by osmosis from your environment, or directly from a specific mentor who has influenced you greatly. You will feel a strong need to get some money together and become more conscientious about what you earn and spend. This ten will force you to think up ways to increase your assets, savings, property or investments and expand in the future so eventually you could provide for your own family. The ten of disks also finds you seeking out a residence where you feel loved, needed and part of a clan, community, tradition or well-established organization.

Your OUTER INFLUENCE is THE STAR, which says you will be extremely happy with how your career and relationships turn out in the end. You will have more self-confidence, physically and emotionally. Your image and personality will attract people who will give you a chance to prove your worth as a worker who shines in their field. You will feel so good about yourself that others will have no choice but to regard you highly. The energy you will radiate will bring light and optimism to everyone you meet. In the future, you will naturally gravitate toward people, organizations and methodologies that you can identify with and perhaps become a leader for later on.

Your HOPE AND FEAR is the TWO OF DISKS, which states that you dread change and all its uncertain manifestations while at the same time you are dying to try something new professionally. This paradox forces you to vacillate between staying and going, and nothing will happen until your present position is terminated or your company closes up shop. This tug-of-war within yourself will be resolved only when you leave your current job or residence. This movement in your life, however, may lead to a squeezed financial situation where you deplete your reserve or have trouble covering your living expenses. Adding to this difficulty is the fact that you want to break free from loneliness and lack of fulfillment and mature emotionally so you can handle more responsibility and get rid of your hesitation toward success.

Your OUTCOME is THE JUGGLER, who is very shrewd when it comes to concealing his personal plans from others so he can secure what he wants for himself. This card stands for you or someone else moving assets around so quickly that nobody knows how much you possess. This trump could depict you becoming a wheeler-dealer in the future. Your natural business abilities will make you quite adept at the deceptive, verbal Ping-Pong that accompanies the ways of commerce. As your outcome, this card emphasizes that you approach all offers coming your way with skepticism. You will figure out the best method for handling your money and career, even if you have to be secretive to be in total control of your life.

THE FOUR CARD SPREAD

WORK AND BUSINESS is the QUEEN OF SWORDS, a calculating and manipulative woman who will offer you a job, tell you of an available position or influence your work situation in a dramatic way. Though she helps you advance profession- ally, she will be very difficult to get along with. Since you are male, and because of the nature of the reading up to this point, this court card seems to indicate a particular female and not you acting in the manner associated with the Queen of swords.

LOVE AND PARTNERSHIP is THE HERMIT, which says you avoid being involved in one close relationship and instead choose to play the role of monk when it comes to mixing with other people. You prefer to be a loner at this time, as freedom from entanglement helps you feel more self-reliant. Your need for independence is the main factor for staying single, but you have to be alone to work out inadequacies in your ability to love another properly before you will be balanced enough to sustain an intimate union with another.

TROUBLE AND CONFLICT is the FIVE OF CUPS, which makes life hard for you emotionally because you are afraid of being hurt as you are oversensitive and easily wounded. You harbor fear and confusion about having a steady partner and are too naive and immature in your response to women. In no way are you ready to be a successful boyfriend as you continue to dwell on your romantic history of never having had a successful long-term union. You really need to establish a trusting bond of friendship with someone of the opposite sex, a friendship that could deepen and become a permanent foundation for building a serious relationship.

MONEY AND MATERIAL MATTERS is the THREE OF CUPS, which suggests a party atmosphere where you approach others in a friendly manner at a social gathering without being concerned if there are any future wives in the crowd. You possess enough money to enjoy the fruits of life, and you take a keen interest in pleasure and recreation. You are having more fun than ever now, though an overwhelming feeling of failure in love tugs at your heart (five of cups). Put aside your disappointment and be grateful for the chance to celebrate the joyful blessings that make your existence seem worthwhile to you.

Reading Five

This reading was given to a female artist who has the Queen of cups as her significator. After years of deliberation she had begun college on full scholarship to specifically study her craft after avoiding this responsibility for most of her adult life. She wanted information about her education and her boyfriend who was paying her living expenses at the time of the reading. The subject-combination of the reading was MONEY AND MATERIAL MATTERS and TROUBLE AND CONFLICT.

THE GRAND CROSS

Your SELF CARD is THE WHEEL OF FORTUNE, which points out that you are a fortunate person right now who can afford to take time to celebrate the access to freedom that has come your way. Many of your daily necessities are taken care of, and you are finally enrolled at the school you have always dreamed of attending without having to pay any tuition. This card describes going with the flow and enjoying the top of the material scale. Let destiny unfold and follow its direction down the path of least resistance where you cannot go wrong and only good awaits you. This is the trump of personal luck, making everything work out for you in the best possible way. With the Wheel as your self card you can do anything you want and must take advantage of opportunities presented to you. Be sure to investigate all plans or offers and act only on those that have the greatest potential for success.

Your PRESENT ENVIRONMENT is

the NINE OF WANDS, which implies seeking security and fighting to keep away negative forces that could harm you or dilute your efforts to develop your creativity. You are not easily approachable, since you defend yourself to avoid personal injury or having the rug pulled out from under you. Your will is directed toward protecting your territory and making your interests number one in your present environment. By doing this you naturally become stronger and more capable of influencing those around you. You want to do more, care more and expend more energy for the survival and flourishing of your talents and abilities. You must feed the artist in you instead of taking time, attention and concentration away from nurturing your work. You are keeping all your wands in place as a fortification to support your current effort to ground yourself and find security.

Your IMMEDIATE OBSTACLE is the EIGHT OF DISKS, which stands for you learning your craft through an apprenticeship that requires you to repeat the same identical task again and again. This aspect of your education is highly useful and the only road to achieving perfection. It is crucial that you concentrate on developing your skills and technique, because the eight of disks is your obstacle. You may be a little hesitant about disciplining yourself so severely at this time, and with the Wheel as your self card, life may be so easy for you that you try to avoid the arduous training of this disk, which emphasizes the necessity for completing your schooling and putting a great deal of time into producing artwork. If you apply yourself diligently and fulfill obligatory assignments, you will reap huge rewards in the future. You could lose sight of your true path should you shirk your creative responsibility, though this seems unlikely with the Wheel as your self card.

Your HOPE AND DREAM is the FIVE OF CUPS, which reveals emotional disappointment either from a relationship that is going sour or from your discovery that school is not fun but hard work (eight of disks). You thought college

would be the perfect way to banish your
discontent, but instead it has forced
more responsibility on you than you ex-
pected. One or two of your dreams are
lost forever, but they would not have
held up in the long run anyway. You should
focus on the cups that remain full and
standing, finding solace in what is
readily available to you. In terms of
love, this card brings friendship to a
union that transcends the frustrating
highs and lows of passionate entanglement
and allows the couple to become true
allies. As this reading concerns money
and trouble, the five says the way
you thought your life would turn out
has not held up to your expectations.
You should seek out those who endured
through thick and thin and let go of
people who have failed you when you
were relying on them. You have to let
go of some of your deepest desires and
follow the most honest and viable goals.
The five of cups is also a card of talents
wasted as you look back in time and
wonder why you did not work hard at
developing your artistic skills before.
You feel a sense of loss over frittering

away your creative energy in the past without producing any pieces you could be proud of.

Your DIFFICULTY IN THE PAST is the TEN OF SWORDS, which shows you coming to the end of a long, tough interval that has exhausted you mentally and drained you physically. This card refers to your daily commute and repetitious life-style of staying up late into the night to do homework, collapsing for a few hours of sleep and getting up early in the morning to travel to school week after week, month after month. What you really need to do is take a brief vacation, which may not be possible. As this card is a sword and a ten, it represents you having thought out every angle of how to make your material situation work out and how to handle the disappointment factor in love. The ten of swords lets you know exactly what the score is, but this card also frustrates you because you lack the strength to change your routine at this time. This spread position proves that your overwhelmed approach to the

trials and tribulations of your creative
destiny (five of cups) has forced you to
the end of your rope intellectually.
You have been tested and stretched
beyond your limits, but you will emerge
victorious from the struggle that will
be your foundation in the days to come.
This sword demands that you encounter
problems along the road to achieving
a true understanding of your personality
and your fate as a soul. This ten can
symbolize a tremendous amount of
knowledge and shows you resynchro-
nizing past life ability by recalling
information that is a natural part of
you and in a sense is your birthright.
It has been hard for you to rediscover
these ancient talents as a craftsperson
because these skills are just now coming
back into your conscious mind through a
slow distillation process. Though you
are aware of your potential, you also
recognize how long and difficult a
path you must follow until you are
ready to apply yourself with total
responsibility to your work, though
this is made easier by the upward
material cycle you are experiencing

with the Wheel. Also you may be confused because you have too many
projects to complete at once due to
your school assignments. This adds
to your feeling of being swamped but
confident as you plan how to take action
to resolve the conflict in your life so
you can concentrate on intellectual
pursuits.

Your LAST OF THE PRESENT is
the KNIGHT OF SWORDS, who swoops
in and brandishes his sword as he goes
after what he wants without considering anyone else. If this card signifies
you, it could indicate that you have
had trouble opening up to the drama
around you and have adopted a mean-
spirited, dominating manner. In the
future you will be less socially with-
drawn and will take a breather from
your struggle for control and accomplishment.
This card could also refer to someone
who played a huge role in your existence
in the recent past, but this spread
points out that his influence over you
is fading fast. This placement could
represent a change in the personality

of whomever you associate this Knight
with in your mind and says that he may
have relinquished his abrasive manner.
In conjunction with the ten of swords
and five of cups, this card would emphasize that the Knight of swords turned
out to be very different in reality from
what you had imagined. Because he does
not want to discuss your relationship,
the problems you two face together
do not have any easy solutions. His
attitude toward you is breaking your
heart and making you suffer, and this,
coupled with your exhausting schedule,
creates much tension for you. You have
lost many of the close, loving feelings
you had for him previously, and your
connection has become weak because
you spend so much time apart. With
the Wheel you are on a roll like never
before, materially, though you still need
to work with the greatest diligence on
the education you have put off to this
point. Meanwhile your friend is acting
like the Knight of swords and is no
longer emotionally available, and although
you have gained much, you have lost
a lot of love along the way. Only the

future will determine whether he will change and whether this phase of alienation is temporary or permanent. Possibly your union will regenerate and improve later on without your training being jeopardized.

Your FIRST OF THE FUTURE is the THREE OF CUPS, which always represents a collective celebration where you enjoy yourself, so expect an invitation to a party or gathering that will change either your career direction or your relationship status. You could meet someone there who could become a powerful and positive force in your life. Even with your exhaustion and responsibilities, you should make an effort to seek out places and people you find relaxing so you can escape for a little while from your endless cycle of personal problems.

Your FUTURE ENVIRONMENT is the FIVE OF WANDS, which indicates that you may be difficult and antagonistic toward others in the coming days. Your actions will start to reflect your deepest passions and highest principles. You may find yourself engaged in arguments that have no resolution to dramatize your discontent with a certain issue. As this wand lies ahead, crossing your path, it symbolizes that you will begin to care so much about the world that you will fight in the name of the good and honorable. You will discover your rightful niche and ultimately surrender your entire existence to its pursuit. Your devotion will guide you in a preordained direction. You are already strong and full of the fire of confidence (nine of wands) as you get the education you deserve, and you are working hard so you can arrive at the proper destination down the road.

Your OUTER INFLUENCE is THE TOWER, which portends that your social arrangements in the future are going to be totally different from what you now think they will be. Your connections with other people will be bigger, better and juicier than you now expect. Some individuals who are currently close to you may leave your life after you see

through their masquerade and decide
to reject them and seek out clear and
honest relationships. The Tower does
not allow you to accept anything at face
value because your eyes are opened up
by the intervention of divine force. You
will have to change plans you thought
were carved in granite but found out later
were flimsy and illusory. Hang on, and
once the clash has ended, you will discover
the best way to proceed in terms of your
involvement in the areas of money and
trouble. The Tower in combination with
the five of cups emphasizes the destruc-
tion of your false expectations and weak
emotional ties so you can sweep away
the debris of your psychological crutch-
es and rebuild through more permanent
people and activities. Due to the three of
swords and the Wheel, this transformation
will liberate you from that which has
imprisoned you for years. You will be
released to follow your spiritual path
with clarity of purpose and a glad
heart brimming over with love once
you are free of alliances and responsibilities that are not really right
for you.

Your HOPE AND FEAR is the FOUR OF WANDS, which hints that your most exalted desire is to have a pleasant home life, and your greatest fear is to have no home life at all. You must eventually find a residence you treasure where you feel comfortable and can welcome anyone you choose. Though your soul cries out for a special place of its own, you do not want to make a move that would jeopardize your relationship. This is a card of social and physical satisfaction, and it suggests promoting calm about the home and reserving your antagonism for your outer world activities in the future (five of wands). You must learn how to temper your destructive behavior so you do not threaten the foundation of your life, though the Tower will force you to replace any cornerstones that are weak. Creatively this card speaks of getting to a point where you can call upon your artistic skills constantly and consistently, though you are fearful of reaching this level of development.

Your OUTCOME is the EIGHT OF

CUPS, which shows that you will totally devote yourself with reverence to a serious path that will bring you great spiritual satisfaction. You will stop focusing on your existential problems, and instead you will become immersed in activities of a more sacred nature. You will mature emotionally, and due to this your struggle with your boyfriend will no longer seem so important, though you will continue to live with him for a while longer. In the end, you may see him as a passing interest, even if you used to think he was your soulmate. Your decision to dedicate yourself to something greater than yourself (eight of cups) will free you in the future and get you over the letdown you experienced with the five of cups. If this relationship is sucked out to sea before the tidal wave of the Tower, your self card implies that any losses will lead to better conditions later on.

THE FOUR CARD SPREAD

WORK AND BUSINESS is the FIVE OF CUPS, which is also your hope and dream.

You are still reeling from an emotional blow, which overshadows the issues of school or employment and has forced you to change your plans. This empty state of soul will pass, but meanwhile you find it hard to focus your attention on the creative victories that have come your way because your heart is crying over good love gone bad. You have to try extra hard not to let disappointment at work deter you from trying something new in the future.

LOVE AND PARTNERSHIP is THE WHEEL, which says that, for whatever reason, the relationship with your boyfriend is lucky for you, though you are hurt by his cold, distant manner. Even with all the difficulties you two have had as a couple, there has been an upward material movement toward fulfillment of your separate destinies. The Wheel as your self card indicates that you are capable of making enough money to support yourself; the nine of wands proves that you could become the main breadwinner in your household. As the Knight of swords, your boyfriend is running scared and scattering his mental energy but is unaware of his own behavior because he is so wrapped up in himself. He will probably continue to avoid any confrontation with you on the issue of healing your alliance, though part of his plan is to live with you and emotionally withdraw from you.

TROUBLE AND CONFLICT is the TWO OF CUPS, which symbolizes the deep mutual attraction you and your friend have for each other, which brought you together originally. The heart connection between you is under great stress due to your current life-style, which keeps you apart most of the time. Also, intimate moments have been lacking from your world, and this has chipped away at the solidarity of feeling you used to share. You still care very much for each other, and loyalty runs thick, which is why you are still united regardless of the constant separations and the alienating lack of communication that is destroying the core of your friendship. The eight of cups in conjunction with the troubled two of cups points out that in the end you will follow the person, cause or work that your soul feels drawn to in the highest sense.

MONEY AND MATERIAL MATTERS is the EIGHT OF WANDS, which depicts money, rewards and recognition coming to you rather quickly. Also, you should be preparing for a ton of chores that will accompany a new project or for taking speedy action to handle a money or business matter. This wand in this position increases your urgency to have cash to spend impulsively without any practical hesitation. This card could indicate you wanting to flee from home and security, especially with the four of wands in the hope and fear position. The nine of wands in your present environment proves you are capable of keeping up with any level of activity with great agility and composure. The five of wands in your future means you will fight for what you believe no matter what the cost is to your already crumbling relationship. As the subject-combination is money

and trouble, the issue of where and
with whom you will live comes down to
whether you can support yourself
financially and stay in school if your
boyfriend is no longer paying your
living expenses.

Reading Six

This reading was given to a male who has
the King of disks as his significator.
He was just starting out on his career
path and wanted to know how to get a
job that would help increase his financial security and aid him in developing
his abilities. The subject-combination of
the reading was TROUBLE AND CONFLICT
and WORK AND BUSINESS.

THE GRAND CROSS

Your SELF CARD is the TWO OF DISKS,
which is a card of change, fluctuating
resources, moving to a new residence or
traveling because it is required by your
line of work. It often indicates trading
in an old job or being indecisive about
staying in one position or trying some-

thing different. No matter where you go or what you do, there is only enough money to cover your expenses, and in no way could you build up any savings. To progress economically, you have to grow materially through the disk suit into the solid three, four, six, nine and ten of disks before the concentrated efforts of the seven and eight can bear fruit with the more resourceful nine and ten of disks. The ace, two and five represent stages of the cupboard being bare for a reason. Right now you find it impossible to gain ground because you are suspended in the limbo of a strained monetary supply and cannot make headway toward better conditions in the future. This leads you to waver back and forth between your choice of paths to follow in life. You should focus on practical matters that need your attention and liberate yourself from uncertainty over your career. The wheels of time are slowly moving you toward your eventual outer world endeavor. On a more mundane level, the two of disks can show you working on two projects at the same time, or it can indicate that your material circumstances are about to undergo a shift or modification. Spiritually the two of disks symbolizes how infinity is composed of cycles that return and repeat again and again forever in universal harmony.

Your PRESENT ENVIRONMENT is JUDGEMENT, which depicts you as the one responsible for your own destiny. You call the shots regarding everything that happens, and when things get bad, you forget that your preincarnated soul designed your struggle to awaken your consciousness to the lessons that are the most important catalysts for enlightenment. All negativity is prearranged to force you to confront major decisions necessary to your evolution. Even though you are making no practical headway with the two of disks, there is great value in the basic business principles you are learning through your present job. You are also judging what your eventual life-style will be as well as your area of career involvement. You are looking at everything through the eyes of truth while remaining firm in your beliefs; you want to do what is right, because you know your behavior has to stand up to eternity. You want to make real what is deeply rooted in the scripture of your psyche. You know now that the only way to ultimate satisfaction in life is being honest at all times and giving of yourself when it is appropriate. Judgement shows you having the gift of seeing through pretenses and not being impressed by superficial status and possessions accumulated at the expense of others. You have the ability to assess people in the naked state of what they really are instead of identifying them by their cultural background, what they own, or whom they know.

Your IMMEDIATE OBSTACLE is the ACE OF DISKS, which is the second disk you have been dealt thus far. The ace and two of disks under the subject-combination of trouble and work emphasize the earliest stages of disk development where you sharpen your skills and generate just enough income to maintain a simple life-style. You are gathering a great deal of information that will be useful to you in your ultimate career choice though you cannot see it now. You are going through a period of learning a little bit about many different things, which is difficult and frustrating because you are not being trained enough in one particular area to have expertise that could help you financially at this time. This ace also symbolizes a forth-coming opportunity whose potential you do not see immediately because you are reluctant to take anything on before you thoroughly investigate it. You could meet someone new and instantly have a negative attitude toward her but in the end she will become a lifetime friend. You do not see her as she is because you are insecure about your place in the world and are too imma-ture and innocent in the ways of business. If you want a successful financial harvest, you must take advantage of every chance you get to develop your abilities. Nurture the growth of these seeds of employment so your bounty will be bigger and better than you have any idea at this time.

Your HOPE AND DREAM is THE LOVERS, which represents relationships based on mutual attraction and reciprocal love. This card could show you having to choose between two different paramours, or this trump could point out that you are tied to someone at work on a deep emotional level. This card can signal that your eventual partner could become a guiding force in your career or a co-worker or collaborator. The card of coupling in this placement is a sign that you are an industrious team player, have great loyalty toward colleagues and employers, and always promote harmony on the job.

Your DIFFICULTY IN THE PAST is THE JUGGLER, which depicts trickery, illusion and deliberate secrecy because you hide information from other people. Keeping up pretenses has been hard for you, but experiencing personal privacy is a crucial lesson for you. This trump allows you to exercise your will to get what you want and teaches you how to utilize silence to draw in the necessary power to stay focused on your spiritual path. This card will serve you

in the future as you continue to conceal
details in order to put yourself ahead
in the game without worrying about the
opinions of others. You now know how
to tune out the world so you can work
unobstructed toward gaining control of
your destiny.

Your LAST OF THE PRESENT is
the FIVE OF CUPS, which symbolizes a
huge disappointment for you in the
recent past because someone or something did not come through, and you
suffered a loss even with the Juggler
giving you the inside angle on things.
Here, three of the cups that were filled
with the liquid equivalent of your ultimate joy have been knocked over and
emptied while two cups remain standing
and full to the brim. You had to let go
of people and situations, and this left
you feeling abandoned and disillusioned.
Any setbacks you have encountered
were educational mistakes designed to
move you forward emotionally because
you are in the earliest stages of
developing your material abilities (ace
and two of disks). You should take

account of what you still possess and make it work for you regardless of how many chances at happiness have already passed you by.

Your FIRST OF THE FUTURE is the ACE OF SWORDS, which in combination with Judgement shows major decisions being initiated in your present environment that will dictate conditions for the rest of your life in the areas of trouble and work. Judgement describes your current job as simply a back road that enables you to deal with a variety of experiences due to the locations of the ace and two of disks in this spread. Though the pay is low (two of disks) you have much to learn about business and are being given the opportunity to do so (ace of disks). The ace of swords indicates that you will rigidly set your mind on pursuing a particular direction, which will help you clarify exactly what you want from your career.

Your FUTURE ENVIRONMENT is the ACE OF WANDS, which stresses

starting over. You have been dealt
three aces so far, which means that you
are definitely beginning a fresh and
important cycle of growth and activity.
With all this pure, inspiring energy
around, you could be tempted to put
the cart before the horse due to your
urge to strike out in many new directions, perhaps before the time is right.
You need to let go of previous disap-
pointments with work, which have left
you emotionally unfulfilled or feeling as
though you have wasted your talents.
You are not using your gifts because
you are at the dawn of blossoming mentally, materially and creatively. You
are not capable of going out on your
own yet due to the presence of two
aces in your future. You are currently
gathering information so you can choose
the right way to pursue the options
you are attracting to yourself through
the ace of disks as your present obstacle. The ace of wands says you will have
all the energy you need to succeed down
the road.

Your OUTER INFLUENCE is the

FOUR OF WANDS, which portrays how other people weave into the fabric of your existence. You will become more socially content later on and will welcome the world into your home with open arms. You will deeply enjoy the fellowship you create within your own four walls as your home becomes head-quarters for those you consider your family and friends. This card denotes a peaceful place where you can renew yourself through the ace of wands in a relaxing and positively charged atmosphere that is conducive to sharing.

Your HOPE AND FEAR is the KNIGHT OF WANDS, which emphasizes movement and maybe having to leave your happy residence, which you adore, in order to travel or relocate to a new environment, though you really just want to stay put. So far in this reading you have two major cards of motion (two of disks and Knight of wands) and have drawn the two most prominent cards of decision-making as well as three cards of new beginnings (aces of disk, sword and wand). The Lovers stands for choosing between two people or ways of being, and its hope and dream position points out how split you are over everyone and everything right now. So there are great changes taking place as you enter a fresh cycle of growth and activity, though the Knight of wands shows you not wanting to leave your job or town, fighting your feelings or running away from encounters. This Knight could also symbolize a man of passionate indecisiveness whom you will deal with in the future, or you could suddenly adopt this sort of behavior.

Your OUTCOME is the ACE OF CUPS, which now gives you all four aces in this spread. This is the card of being in love and overflowing with the pure joy only a genuine caring friendship brings into your life. Your ultimate choice of career will be something you feel strongly about, or your love relationship will be at the heart of it, or you may depart from your present location to be with your girl-friend. The watery ace of cups and

the fiery ace of wands are always
associated with receptive sexual
energy and creative aggressive drive.
Both these cards show that your
attraction to your girlfriend is funda-
mentally physical, and the Lovers
clearly states that you hold this person
above all others. This union is crucial
to your destiny as a worker in the world
and creates a foundation from which
you build emotionally and professionally.
The issue is whether you will develop
all your inherent ability (symbolized
by the four aces in this spread) and
where you should establish your residence and place of business, though the
four of wands says that you will be
quite content with your eventual home
situation. It seems definite that you
will follow your partner because you
are deeply connected to her and in a
sense cannot live without her (the
Lovers and aces of wand and cup).
At this time you are truly together, heart
and soul, and you challenge each other
to grow stronger and become better
people daily. Also, be prepared for increased social activity, which will add

an element of fun to the common routines of your life that are a bore when done solo.

THE FOUR CARD SPREAD

WORK AND BUSINESS is THE WHEEL OF FORTUNE, which indicates luck is on your side concerning your career. You are extremely fortunate when it comes to finding jobs that pay well, and you make enough money to afford a quality lifestyle even though you live simply. You could reach the top of your chosen field if you take advantage of the opportunities that cross your path. Your hard work will be rewarded because the Wheel promises this to you. Paying your dues now will bring you success when the timing is right. You will be shown the way to the perfect occupation that would afford you more sociability and financial security. You are being given a fantastic chance to make some cash, enjoy your routine and adopt a highly independent life-style. You need room to become yourself and be triumphant in actualizing your potential. Get ready to rise to the occasion when the Wheel turns in your favor because there is no better Tarot card for the work position, and its presence assures you of total satisfaction and joyful prosperity.

LOVE AND PARTNERSHIP is JUSTICE, which is always a card of legalities. In this Four Card Spread placement, it emphasizes the laws or rules that specifically apply to formalized relationships between people. If you are considering getting married, you may face a prenuptial agreement to protect the interests of both parties by establishing an equitable distribution of assets should you divorce. If you are going into business with someone, Justice would suggest lawyers, contracts, licenses and much paperwork to spell out the financial rights and responsibilities of everyone involved. On a much higher level, this trump represents a love alliance that requires fairness and compromise between two people in an effort to heal mutual karma from past experiences together. Justice challenges you to treat someone you feel strongly about either positively or negatively with respect and equanimity.

TROUBLE AND CONFLICT is the PAGE OF DISKS, a card of studying or undertaking an apprenticeship. This may stand for attending school, but more often it symbolizes being shown the ropes or put through the paces of learning a trade, skill or know-how behind a particular business. You need to apply yourself now so in the future you can own a venture, keep the books, administer the paperwork and negotiate all legal procedures for a company. Justice warns you to be careful of anything you sign and to employ the best counsel if you enter into agreements with any other party. The Page of disks forces you to get involved with every aspect of an enterprise so you could run one yourself later on.

MONEY AND MATERIAL MATTERS is THE SUN, which spreads warmth and happiness to every corner of your material world. You may be thinking of moving to a tropical, warmer or more southerly environment where you could blissfully establish a home and a work routine that would be directly related to the climate being sunny and perhaps resortlike. You are realizing with a brilliant clarity that you must go to such a place in order to make your existence fulfilling. You are totally aware of the line of employment you would like to pursue to generate income, and your devotion to achieving happiness will lead you to your ultimate occupation and life-style. First you need to undergo a rigorous training or apprenticeship to one or more expert individuals due to the position of the Page of disks, though you are reluctant to give up the next few years to be an assistant to an employer rather than be an executive yourself. The presence of all four aces in this reading emphasizes that you must develop your talents (disks), ideas (swords), intuition (cups) and creativity (wands) if you are going to make good use of your current destiny.

Reading Seven

This reading was given to a male artist who had relocated far from home and was having trouble getting work done, which made him wonder whether he had done the right thing. He also wanted to know how he could produce marketable artwork that would sell and support him financially. By moving he had left behind a long-standing, unfulfilling relationship that had continually gotten in the way of his career. The subject-combination was TROUBLE AND CONFLICT and LOVE AND PARTNERSHIP.

THE GRAND CROSS

Your SELF CARD is Jupiter, which shows you understanding the symbolic value of the scenes and sequences of your life. You have reached a point in your evolution where you know how to interpret people and everyday events in terms of their spiritual importance. Jupiter also speaks of tapping the mysterious world of dreams and the subconscious, which are an integral part of the great collec-

tive memory that contains an impression
of moments in history explained through
the wisdom of universal law. All
artists forge their own hieroglyphics,
which are both personal and cosmologi-
cal. Your knowledge sets you apart
from the crowd because you are not a
victim of the artificial subliminal lures
of society, glamour and greed, which
are traps to trip you on the path to
learning the truth about yourself. Due
to your metaphysical focus, you are
bored and distracted when it comes to
material pursuits because they seem so
trivial to enlightened Jupiter. As this
is the card of the teacher, you may be
thinking about becoming an educator to
pass on your insights and abilities to
others. You could be in training for this
now, and you can be sure this is a positive step to take. The benevolence of
the planet Jupiter brings expansion and
opportunity to you if you have done your
homework and seek soul-satisfying
rewards. As this reading is love and
trouble, this trump finds you interested
in a higher level of attraction with
another rather than a purely temporal,

physical connection. This card could show you currently offering a platonic relationship to someone because you do not want to become intimate until you have slowly investigated whether this person is just a passing archetype in the parade of women who pass through your daily existence. Jupiter can speak of being subconsciously drawn to a person whose image, energy or voice reminds you of one who had a tremendous effect on you in your past.

Your PRESENT ENVIRONMENT is the FOUR OF WANDS, the card of the happy home. You derive a great deal of pleasure from the place where you live and the people you hang out with in your day-to-day life. You are thrilled to have your home and always look forward to returning there after a trip away from your base. You enjoy including others in your activities, even though high-minded Jupiter points out your slightly detached, holier-than-thou energy right now. The four of wands is a stabilizing force that helps you decide where and how and with whom to live so you can feel safe and complete in your home environment. You may also be trying to get your passionate nature under control by zeroing in on one particular person. If you are not in a relationship presently, you are realizing that you want to relax and feel comfortable with the woman you get involved with next time around.

Your IMMEDIATE OBSTACLE is the THREE OF SWORDS, which suggests sorrow due to separation from someone you care about, and this is affecting your ability to enjoy the four of wands atmosphere around you with the wisdom of Jupiter behind you. You miss this person terribly, and her absence is a block in your heart. This sword pictures you reaching a depth of melancholy that will push you to create works based on that which moves your soul. You are always aware of being apart from the one who preoccupies your mind. As an obstacle, this card is interfering with the satisfaction and contentment you should be feeling due to functioning on a higher frequency with more regularity than ever before (Jupiter). You are unable to have a normal pleasurable social life because you are mentally focused on a person or matter distracting you from your daily activities.

Your HOPE AND DREAM is the PAGE OF DISKS, which implies that more than anything you want to gather knowledge and ability. You may get involved with a group of people or one particular mentor who will help you expand your education as would a teacher for a student. This Page reiterates your desire to study your field of interest and points to the necessity for training before you can really do anything at all. You should begin to put your thoughts down in written form and perhaps keep a journal so you can record your ideas, impressions and accumulated wisdom. You need to apply yourself to all your tasks with great diligence toward your chosen discipline if you want to achieve your hope and dream of being a talented, dependable artist. This Page can refer to cataloging your collection of work to date by sorting through your pieces, labeling them, and accounting for each and every sketch, painting, sculpture and drawing in a logical manner. The three of swords also speaks of the wheeling and dealing you must endure with those in the art world who could assist you in getting some recognition, though up to this point your colleagues have been silent or brutally critical of your work. And the disk Page always needs more experienced people telling him what to do and guiding him through business matters.

Your DIFFICULTY IN THE PAST is THE EMPRESS, who is usually a fountain of inspiration but in this placement suggests the trouble you have had finding a fruitful source of creativity in the past. Your artistic output was produced in short, frenzied bursts of great intensity but never by toiling daily year-round. This card can signify a woman who teaches or stimulates you, but her powerful, sensuous personality is a problem for you, and though you need her as a muse and mentor, it is hard for you to accept your feelings for her. In the future, she will remain extremely supportive of you, and her nurturing role will continue.

Your LAST OF THE PRESENT is TEMPERANCE, which proves you have mastered divine patience after having waited a long time for conditions to be right for action. The influence of this card is now leaving your life, but it has transformed and balanced every area of your existence. During this interval, you had to control displaying your affection for someone and alternately acted hot and cold toward this person. The way you have been relating to others in general has been unpredictable at best. You are also finishing a period of improving yourself physically, mentally and spiritually in an effort to live as simply and as naturally as possible. You have had to cut away at eccentricities in your personality so you can settle down to do some serious work (Page of disks) and are not overly concerned with outward appearances

and superficial differences (Jupiter). All
you want right now is to become connected to people and organizations in
your field of interest.

Your FIRST OF THE FUTURE is
the PAGE OF CUPS, which is the first
cup in this Grand Cross; so far you have
three trumps, one sword, one wand
and one disk. This Page could indicate
those who sell your art for a percentage
of the profits or someone who works
with you as a capable assistant, co-
worker or partner. Whether it represents you or another, this card displays
a shy, gentle, passive, earnest and
industrious person who is naive and insecure about his professional status.
This Page could also characterize a
young adoring figure who becomes attached to you in a sweet but slightly
annoying way.

Your FUTURE ENVIRONMENT is
the KNIGHT OF SWORDS, who overlooks
or ignores the best things in life and
needs to slow down and take a more
active part in the world instead of

viewing others as getting in the pathway of his self-centered goals. He has no interest in anyone but himself and uses his sword to force people out of his picture by neither listening to them nor acknowledging their presence. If the truth be known, he is basically unstable mentally and emotionally. In the future, you will be influenced by the behavior of such a person or you may begin to act in this manner to fulfill your ambitions as soon as possible.

Your OUTER INFLUENCE is THE JUGGLER, which says you will decide not to let anyone know what you are doing. You will keep things to yourself to ensure the success of what you want to accomplish with this powerful trump. People will wonder why you suddenly stopped communicating, where you live and how you move around day to day. You may employ furtive methods soon to protect a secret or scandal from those around you. This is also a card of intuitive awareness where you use insight to forecast the outlook for your family, friends, partners and associates.

On a higher level, the Juggler shows you bearing the responsibility for the consequences of all your actions through the force field of karma you have built up in the past.

Your HOPE AND FEAR is the ACE OF SWORDS, which will compel you to make a specific decision, perhaps against your own intentions. This ace says that standing firm and being resolute in mind will help you cut through the draining but enhancing sensitivity of the three of swords and liberate you from the heavy thoughts and feelings that are weighing you down. For some strange reason, you are afraid to let go of your melancholy and come to a point of controlling your emotions so you can be more directed toward what you truly want. The Knight of swords as your future environment in combination with the Juggler reiterates the theme of complete determination, which is weakened only by the poor placement of the three of swords in its annoying position. By analyzing these swords you can get a

sense of where you are heading intellectually in terms of what this spread means
in your life.

Your OUTCOME is the QUEEN OF
WANDS, who, like the Empress, represents an active, creative, courageous
woman who knows what she wants and
how to get it. She is very sharp and
usually outspoken but soulful because
as a wand she has a pure heart under-
neath her armor, whereas the Queen
of swords battles on an almost exclu-
sively mental level. This reading also
contains the four of wands, which
symbolizes comfort and contentment,
courtesy of the Queen of wands in
the future. You may ultimately put
your life in her hands if she becomes
your choice from the array of potential
partners. Because you are trying to
stabilize your passionate nature through
this four, you want to be true to her;
but the location of the ace of swords
shows great indecision or hesitation
about her imminent role in your destiny. As your subject-combination is
trouble and love, you could end up with

her, but this would not come about easily.
You are experiencing distance or separation from her (three of swords), and though
you remain philosophically detached
from the matter (Jupiter), you are
fairly happy (four of wands) and just
want to produce some solid, meaningful
work (Page of disks), a goal that has
eluded you in the past. You have had
some difficulty channeling ideas and
imagery by connecting with your source
of inspiration or your ideal mate (the
Empress). You have just come through
a time period of balancing your personality and life-style and learning to
be unnaturally patient (Temperance).
Emotionally you will be vulnerable in
the future but will deal with these
feelings by fighting fiercely for your
own interests (Knight of swords),
knowing you will have to make a specific
decision about an issue or relationship
when your choice will dictate your path
in life (ace of swords). During this
process you will not share your plans,
thoughts or emotions with anyone else
(the Juggler). At this point it looks
as though you may walk off with the

Queen of wands, though you treat her with an indifference only the Knight of swords and the Juggler can project. You realize following her is the way to go, and yet you hide your desire for her from everyone, especially her. She would be a demanding partner who would keep you on your toes, but she is also a relaxing mate who has a surprisingly warm, caring nature. The Empress and the Queen of wands may even refer to the same woman in this spread.

THE FOUR CARD SPREAD

WORK AND BUSINESS is the KING OF CUPS, a card of commerce taking place overseas or internationally with negotiations between people from different countries. This King can also be symbolic of someone who does not appear interested in your work but is actually intensely affected by it and is hiding any feelings he has about working with you. The King of cups can indicate a dominant individual who directly influences your career and can make it easier or more difficult, depending on how you interpret what he teaches you. He could represent an agent, gallery owner, parent, partner or employer who has the power to move mountains for you. This King is always distant because he controls his emotions; if this card characterizes your behavior, it shows you inhibiting your feelings and trying to take charge of your own business by expanding your number of projects.

LOVE AND PARTNERSHIP is THE UNIVERSE, which implies that an evolved relationship for you is inevitable, and you are moving toward it as fast as you can. This is a card of letting time pass so you can mature enough to be ready for a union based on mutual attraction of mind, body and spirit, which carries on by its own inner momentum year after year, getting better every day. This is the most exalted of partnerships and represents nothing short of meeting your soulmate in reality. Not having this type of connection troubles you, and you spend a great deal of time and expend much energy in your search for the right woman.

TROUBLE AND CONFLICT is the EIGHT OF CUPS, which says you want to drop everything to follow something you believe in that evokes a deep, solemn emotion, satisfying the longing of the three of swords. You are seriously looking to be shown the way to a true understanding of your purpose in life so you can direct yourself toward that which your soul already strives for with Jupiter as your self card. This cup describes how hard it is for you to begin a quest for the path that would align itself with the chord of your being and would reveal your inner light. You should prepare for this journey toward enlightenment by getting ready to shift into a twenty-four-hour existence devoted to your work, which will be difficult due to this spread position. The eight of cups shows your every thought, feeling, dream and action dominated by the issues that the reading discusses.

MONEY AND MATERIAL MATTERS is the TEN OF WANDS, which pictures a period of time when you shoulder a huge burden out of duty or loyalty. You accomplish a great deal for the benefit of yourself and others and take your material responsibilities to heart. Due to the placement of this card, people may depend on you emotionally and financially, which is a drain on your energy supply. You find yourself dragged down by money problems and are overloaded with accountability to the breaking point. This is a hardship for you, and you often feel as though you lack a purpose of your own, although nothing could be further from the truth. Like the Knight of swords, you are unable to see where you are headed and therefore cannot make gains in your field of interest, which is all you really want to do (Page of disks as your hope and dream). The tens are the end of the line of their suit; the ten of wands denotes maximum caring that supports people and helps them make situations work out in their favor. This wand prevents you from saying no to others and taxes your strength as you attempt to take care of your own needs while those to whom you have a karmic tie require you to play the role of provider.